The Retreat of Globalisation

Anticipating radical change in the culture of financial markets

Every owner of a physical copy of

The Retreat of Globalisation

can download the eBook for free direct from us at Harriman House, in a DRM-free format that can be read on any eReader, tablet or smartphone.

Simply head to:

ebooks.harriman-house.com/retreat

to get your copy now.

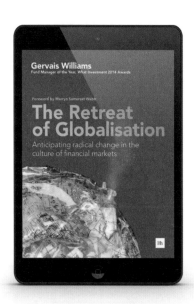

The Retreat
of Globalisation

Anticipating radical change in the culture
of financial markets

Gervais Williams

Hh

HARRIMAN HOUSE LTD
18 College Street
Petersfield
Hampshire
GU31 4AD
GREAT BRITAIN
Tel: +44 (0)1730 233870
Email: contact@harriman-house.com
Website: www.harriman-house.com

First published in Great Britain in 2016
Copyright © Gervais Williams

Paperback ISBN: 978-0-85719-575-3
eBook ISBN: 978-0-85719-576-0

British Library Cataloguing in Publication Data
A CIP catalogue record for this book can be obtained from the British Library.

Typeset by Harriman House.
Written with Mary Ziegler.
Exhibit and cover design by Stephen Taylor, Heat Design.

For Lucas, Ella and Poppy

Contents

List of Figures   ix

Acknowledgements   xi

FOREWORD BY
Merryn Somerset Webb   xiii

Introduction   1

CHAPTER ONE:
The World as We Know it   3

CHAPTER TWO:
The Strange Case of Corporate Profits   15

CHAPTER THREE:
The Age of Plenty   23

CHAPTER FOUR:
The Second Major Credit Boom   31

CHAPTER FIVE:
The Balance Between Growth and Decay   43

CHAPTER SIX:
A Profits Recession   51

CHAPTER SEVEN:
Aggregate Risks   59

CHAPTER EIGHT:
Turn and Face the Change   69

CHAPTER NINE:
Niche is Nice   81

CHAPTER TEN:
Productivity Improvement   85

CHAPTER ELEVEN:
Superior Service Standards for Superior Returns   91

CHAPTER TWELVE:
Risk Reduction   97

CONCLUSION:
The Changing Face of Finance   103

Bibliography   113

Index   117

List of Figures

Exhibit 1: The power of low-cost imports 10

Exhibit 2: Notional drivers of the substantial rise in equity prices 17

Exhibit 3: Surging capital flows 18

Exhibit 4: The rise in US corporate profits 20

Exhibit 5: The slump in UK households' savings ratio 22

Exhibit 6: Global mergers and acquisitions 25

Exhibit 7: China's growing share of world trade 32

Exhibit 8: Chinese capital expenditure 35

Exhibit 9: The scale of the Chinese credit boom 39

Exhibit 10: The slump in UK productivity 49

Exhibit 11: UK: Real wages under pressure 55

Exhibit 12: UK equities: Dividend cover recovered strongly following the crisis in 2008   62

Exhibit 13: UK equities: Dividend cover has greatly deteriorated   65

Exhibit 14: The remarkable decline in UK long bond yields   71

Exhibit 15: An iceberg of dissatisfaction   94

Acknowledgements

I enjoyed writing the acknowledgements for this book because it's the product of an unusually able and hardworking team. I am just one part of that team, and without their skill and effectiveness there wouldn't be a book at all.

Mary Ziegler and Stephen Taylor have already demonstrated their strengths on my two previous books. I was so grateful that they were able to juggle their commitments and help me out once again. Their agility and competence in getting this book over the line is more than exemplary. As in the previous books, Mary has worked with me on the text of the book. She has not only brought in new content but also provided more context to the central ideas. In addition I know the key facts quoted in the book are double-checked, so the main argument of the book rests on solid foundations. Stephen is brilliant at book covers and internal artwork. Often business books have dull illustrations but Stephen's are always a good mix of both the engaging and the informative.

I also recommend potential writers consider Harriman House as their publisher. It's so easy to work well with Chris Parker, Myles Hunt and the rest of the team.

It is always important that the technical facts in a book like this are accurate, because otherwise the credibility of the arguments is undermined. In my experience, Andrew Hunt has been on the button regarding forthcoming economic trends since 1990. Once again he very kindly ensured the economic argument was cogent, and helped supply some of the exhibits within the text. Alongside Andrew, Julien Garran of The

MacroStrategy Partnership very kindly read and reread a couple of drafts of the text and provided some extra examples of the trends discussed in the book. I haven't known Julien or his colleagues, Andy Lees and James Ferguson, as long as I have known Andrew Hunt, but their economic insights are equally brilliant. I tend to feel I need not read anything else after having read Andrew Hunt's and MacroStrategy's reports.

My colleagues at Miton have continued to be hugely supportive and helpful in getting the book to read well. Charlotte Cuthbertson spent many hours reading and rereading the drafts to provide editorial input, and suggested improvements to the flow of the arguments. She has also taken a leadership role to ensure all the events around the launch of the book are well coordinated with my admittedly tight schedule. In addition, Philip Ost read an early draft, marked up many suggested changes and provided plenty of encouragement. Martin Turner, Bart Edgar, Andy Jackson and Niall Coyne also suggested some significant changes that were adopted straightaway. I have also had plenty of help from those outside Miton, with Charles Conner in particular adding some great comments.

Melissa Gilmour generously took on the role of publicising the book, despite having many other commercial commitments. Her enthusiasm is infectious, and she appears to have unlimited energy in arranging launch events, websites, YouTube videos, media appearances and the like. I have always believed I have quite a high work ethic, but I have to accept that I have more than met my match in the extraordinarily pacy work completed by Melissa.

Finally I would like to thank Merryn Somerset Webb for agreeing to write the foreword. The book finally came together rather suddenly, and she turned her thoughts around in an equally tight time frame.

As you can see, this book has been produced with the help of a strong team. It moved from being an idea into a finished book extraordinarily quickly at the end. There won't be many authors luckier than me with this team around them.

Gervais Williams, December 2016

Merryn Somerset Webb

This will go down as the decade in which the world started to build walls. During the 2016 US presidential campaign, much horror was expressed in Europe over Donald Trump's plans to fence the open bits of the US/Mexico border. But for some time before America started listening to a word Trump said, anyone looking from the US to the EU could easily have had a head start on this kind of horror. In 2012 Greece built a fence along its border with Turkey. There has been a major upgrade to the barriers around the French entrance to the Eurotunnel. In 2015 Austria built a fence against Slovenia. Now it is proposing one along its border with Italy. Hungary has completed a barrier between it and Serbia and like Slovenia has built one on its border with Croatia. Ukraine and Estonia want to build walls between them and Russia. When we are done with all this there will be more physical barriers in Europe than there were during the Cold War.

These are the physical signs of what Gervais calls the retreat of globalisation. But there are other less visible ones. Goods are about to get the same treatment as people. Trump isn't keen on free trade – but then again neither were any of the other candidates hoping to be US president in 2017. The EU likes to think it is keen on free trade but it isn't having much luck making deals: its constituent countries just aren't as into it as their leaders think they should be. The CETA between the

EU and Canada barely made it through its last round of negotiation (after seven years!). The UK is renegotiating its trade deals with Europe. The Transatlantic Trade and Investment Partnership looks dead in the water. Further afield so does the Trans-Pacific Partnership, and NAFTA – the deal between the US, Canada and Mexico – looks unlikely to last a Trump presidency in its current form. All in all, according to research organisation Global Trade Alert, protectionist measures were up 50% in 2015 year-on-year, with initiatives harming foreign commercial interests outnumbering liberalisation initiatives by three to one.

Capital might be next in line for a forced retreat. Moving money around the world isn't as easy as it used to be: informal barriers are all over the place (try opening a bank account in a foreign country...) and governments talk about capital controls with an ease that would have been unthinkable in the 1990s. So much for the freedom of movement of capital, goods and people we think of as being crucial to global growth.

This seemed so unlikely even a decade ago. Then it seemed that a clear consensus had been reached: liberal democracy and open borders were all that were needed for the whole world to get rich. So what's gone wrong?

The answer is that while globalisation has been brilliant in aggregate – lifting millions out of horrible poverty and doing miracles for global GDP – it also created a class of left-behinds, something that a series of credit bubbles covered up until the financial crisis, but can cover up no more. The existence of these left-behinds – mainly those who, pre-globalisation, would have had middle-income-style jobs (skilled manufacturing, administration and clerical) – means that in the end globalisation has to clash with national democracy. After all, if you live and work in America's Midwest and you lose your job as manufacturing is outsourced to Mexico or China, what's it to you if comparative advantage means that the world as a whole has more cars and coffee makers than it might have otherwise? How much can a cheap smartphone and endless internet really compensate you for the loss of life purpose? And how much more galling is your situation when you know that while globalisation has made you rather poorer than you think you might have been, it has made the global elite disgustingly richer?

Look at it like that and the turn should come as no particular surprise to politicians. It also shouldn't be too much of a surprise to investors. For the last 30 years the onward march of globalisation has allowed the world's big companies to have pretty much everything their own way. Their labour costs have collapsed. Their money has been all but free. They have paid tax where they felt like it (and often in the amounts that suited them) and they have found their goods welcome pretty much everywhere. It's been lovely for them. But, as anyone who has even the faintest faith in mean-reversion will know, all good things come to an end. And all these are.

As democracy begins to intervene, our global companies are set to find out just how sovereign countries can be when they feel like it and how fast the social tide can turn. You can see the change in the new walls. You can see it in the protests against executive pay, in the demands that employees be allowed to sit on boards; in the votes to raise the minimum wage that were also on several state ballots in the US election; and in the EU's plans to introduce new higher tariffs on anyone thought to be selling unfairly priced goods in their markets. Trump's election may just have marked peak globalisation. So what next? In this beautifully timed book, Gervais tells us that you will need to change your investment strategies more over the next three years than you have over the last three decades if you want to be one of the relatively few investors that survive peak globalisation with intact assets. How? Read on.

Introduction

For most of us, cultural norms appear to be just that – norms. But collective attitudes fluctuate far more than most appreciate. Examples litter history: public hanging only ended in the UK because it became too popular.

The fact is that social attitudes change considerably – and it pays to be alert as to when they do. Globalisation has been running into headwinds for a while but until recently few have appreciated that it has already passed its high-water mark. With the benefit of hindsight, we can now see Brexit in the context of a new social trajectory. The election of Donald Trump as the president of the United States underlines this new bearing.

The same holds true in finance – perhaps even more so. Markets have already entered a period of flux. Social disenchantment with globalisation was already a political issue. But the market implications of a retreat from globalisation remain greatly under-appreciated. It's a bit like the game at children's parties where you try to decipher an image from a tiny fragment of the whole – it's hard to recognise the full picture at close range.

Extraordinarily low bond yields don't just mean it is less costly to borrow – they also imply that future returns will be very modest.

Previously I have highlighted just how much several credit boom decades have distorted investor norms. *Slow Finance* and *The Future is Small* outlined investment strategies that could be expected to outperform while world growth was slowing.

But now we are past the turn and economic trends have changed decisively. Now we can be more confident that future market trends will be *very* different from past decades – it will be like moving from the vigour of a rainforest to the seasonal cycles of a temperate woodland.

Get ready for economic cycles to reappear. Summer – winter – summer – winter… And get ready for more company setbacks. The corporate world will once again become a more even mix of growth and decay.

When there is more corporate decay about, financial averages lose their appeal. Index funds are already passing their sell-by date. It is time to be more decisive and a lot more selective. It's going to become more important to actively select the best stocks for your capital. But how can investors know what might constitute the best stocks? *The Retreat of Globalisation* argues for some unconventional yardsticks going forward.

The answers may seem counter-intuitive to those who have only known one set of economic conditions. But the need to find those answers has never been more pressing. Investment strategies will change more in the next three years than they have changed in the past three decades.

CHAPTER ONE:

The World as We Know it

Liberalising trade and deregulating the debt and financial markets – this is how the credit boom in developed markets was born.

An endangered status quo

It's an age-old problem. Most long-term savers are willing to tolerate some risk to generate attractive returns. Yet fluctuating markets undermine their confidence, raising questions as to whether their capital is invested in the right kinds of assets.

So equity investing comes with anxiety. Is it a good time to invest now or is it better to wait for a while? Which parts of the markets could come through with the best long-term returns? In the end, most investors project long-term trends from the past into the future. Generally this approach has worked well over the last few decades. Markets may react minute by minute to every bit of news, but the underlying trajectory of the financial world typically reflects dominant social and economic trends – and these can be consistent for decades.

Consider the market returns since the 1980s. Over recent decades, returns on all assets – from houses through to stocks and shares – have come in well above inflation.[1] There may have been setbacks but these have all been followed by strong recoveries. Indeed, for those with uninvested capital each major setback has marked an excellent time to step up investment – and participate in even better returns as markets rally from the bottom.

The best investment strategy for decades has been to back the status quo.

But there's a problem – social trends *aren't* as consistent as most assume. The status quo is anything but stable over the longer term. Occasionally social (and by implication economic) trends surprise everyone by an abrupt move in a completely new direction.

It all starts when a new meme in our collective psyche germinates. But in the early years, new social trends are often discounted because so many new ideas simply peak out and disappear without ever becoming mainstream. Market noise also frequently distracts market participants from appreciating that trends might be changing. In fact, radical social change often looks unviable because it simply seems inconceivable for attitudes to diverge so far from the consensus. Even when a change becomes more established, many continue to ignore it. Who wants to abandon the status quo when forthcoming trends are not yet fully formed?

So it is only when a change in social attitudes becomes so well-established that it overwhelms the previous status quo that it is fully appreciated. At this stage it seems to have appeared from nowhere, bursting onto the scene fully fledged. The truth, of course, is that change has been coming through for some time, but for a long period it has not been recognised or understood.

The problem with substantive changes like this is that there are so many false starts. Substantive change just doesn't happen very often. And often it's only with the perspective of time that we can fully appreciate how abrupt changes in our social attitudes tend to drive similarly abrupt changes in the long-term trends in markets.

---

1   Recently, of course, the commodity sell-off has undermined returns for this asset class, but the long-term trend has been broadly upwards.

With this in mind, it pays to be alert when social attitudes morph. The major changes tend be more radical than most appreciate, and can initiate changes that are fundamental to dominant economic and market trends. For most of the time it is sensible to remain sceptical, because substantial social change occurs so infrequently. It is worth sitting back to see if a new meme really has proper resilience and momentum – to see if it is capable of gathering increasingly wide-ranging support. New ideas are normally found wanting. The status quo tends to remain the status quo.

But just occasionally the stars align and an abrupt change in social attitudes really does occur. The implications for markets are always significant.

Politics and social change

So what are the best areas to monitor for impending social (and therefore economic) change?

In a democracy, the political world is one such area. In politics, different perspectives are constantly being contested. New ideas are always being discussed. The centre ground in political and economic policy usually holds sway – but there are always those with different views. Divergent ideas and voices vie together in a melting pot of potential new social trends.

Political trends are also easy to monitor and, thanks to the ballot box in elections and referendums, are constantly being tested for conviction.

Sometimes a political development seems to catch the moment – in the 1970s in the UK there was a sudden surge in support for a new party called the SDP. Similarly, on a smaller scale, enthusiasm grew for the UK's Green Party over the past 10–15 years. However, new parties rarely gain serious traction. After merging with the SDP, the Liberal Party might have changed its name to the Liberal Democrats, and when the Green Party was gaining votes the Conservative Party might have changed its logo to a green tree. But the political consensus remained largely consistent.

Just occasionally, things are different.

The last decade has witnessed extraordinary growth in support for the Scottish National Party. This is no mere SDP-style brief surge. The SNP hasn't just grown to become the largest party in Scotland – it has almost entirely displaced the previous incumbent. In the 2010 UK general election six SNP MPs were elected; in 2015, the number was 54. (There remain only five other Scottish MPs.)

Meanwhile, a routine change in the leadership of the Labour Party after the 2015 general election resulted in an overwhelming win for an unconventional politician who was only included on the ballot as a paper tiger. Labour MPs were so stunned by Jeremy Corbyn's victory that they organised a repeat leadership contest in 2016. But new social attitudes have become resilient: the previous result was underlined with an even larger winning margin – despite the fact that Jeremy Corbyn isn't especially charismatic.

Political change like this is instructive. But is it substantive enough to indicate the displacement of a previous political consensus – the harbinger of deep and profound social change?

The SNP may rule the roost in Scotland but the referendum on independence fell short of a full majority. Polling remains ambiguous about support for Scottish independence more than two years on. Jeremy Corbyn might have been re-elected to his party's leadership on an even greater majority than before – but polls indicate that the general public has less appetite for a government led by the Labour Party than at any time since the 1990s.

In isolation, perhaps these examples could be dismissed as the kind of social change that needs to be closely monitored rather than acted upon – political fluctuations that may not persist in the form of long-term social change.

But they are part of a broader and accelerating trend – the reaction to globalisation. It can be seen in Jeremy Corbyn's Labour and in the 'hard Brexit' MPs of Theresa May's Conservatives, in enthusiasm for the SNP on one side of the Atlantic and the victory of Donald Trump on the other. Not to mention the improving political fortunes of nationalist politicians in France, Austria, Hungary and elsewhere.

The fact that it is reflected in so many diverse political developments shows that it is not a question of nationalism alone. Note that it embraces both right- and left-wing parties, which demonstrates that it is not a passing swing of the political pendulum either.

The UK was first to indicate the scale of the rotation in social norms during 2016. During June the UK electorate was offered the opportunity to determine whether it would remain part of the EU. The media consensus assumed that the so-called 'Brexit' referendum held that summer would be an interesting debate, but ultimately that society would remain little changed. Instead the vote revealed that British society had *already* changed. The electorate was keener to vote for the unknown in millions than to stick with the status quo.

This marked a profound change: confounding politicians, pundits, pollsters and even betting markets, more than 17 million British people voted to leave the EU, a margin of victory of over 1.3 million votes.

Some dispute the intentions behind the vote for Brexit – there are almost as many arguments as there are voters – but it is hard to dispute that a vote which displaces the status quo is not a revolt against that status quo.

International markets initially dismissed Brexit as a one-off event. But the nature of the change has real depth and weight. The social trajectory has changed much more profoundly than most anticipated. The election of Donald Trump as president of the United States was the defining moment. One data point could be dismissed as an outlier; two mark a new trend.

The evidence is now overwhelming that social attitudes towards globalisation are undergoing deep change across the developed world. The change may still be immature, and as yet it is unknown how far these changes will come through in legislatures. It may be that Corbyn's Labour never see power; Brexit may not end up being 'hard' and Scotland may never be independent. But don't count on it. The new direction of travel is now obvious. We have entered a period of profound social and therefore economic upheaval. We are on the cusp of a period of multi-decade change.

This is a time for investors to be attentive – very attentive.

The last great change

Social change can influence the trends in financial markets in such significant ways that it is a good idea to circle back to when the UK last underwent a major change in social attitudes.

It took place in the 1970s. Some readers may even be able to remember the scale of dissatisfaction at the time. The UK was a troubled economy. Inflation was a perennial problem. Industrial relations were dreadful. The UK was labelled the 'sick man of Europe'. Everybody was unsettled.

The political consensus favoured restricting imports of low-cost goods because unrestricted imports from lower-cost producers would undermine the viability of local manufacturers. Countries with higher wages, such as the UK, naturally had higher labour costs, so many manufacturing industries simply weren't viable if they were undercut by lower-cost goods imported freely from elsewhere. Prior to the 1980s, exporters from emerging economies with lower unit costs were routinely saddled with import tariffs, preserving the viability of Western manufacturing jobs.

It is interesting to note the parallels between today and the mid-1970s. The UK joined the European Economic Community (the precursor to the EU) in 1973, with a national referendum then held to confirm the decision in 1975 (67% voted to stay in). In the same year, Margaret Thatcher (like Jeremy Corbyn) surprised political pundits by winning the leadership of her party.

Even prior to the 1980s, there was evidence that social attitudes were in a period of flux. With the benefit of hindsight we can see that economists had convinced the electorate and politicians that a significant reduction in international trade barriers would result in a wide-ranging increase in wealth creation. Although less-restricted imports of low-cost goods might lead to job losses in some industries, it was anticipated that those reductions would be more than offset by higher-wage jobs created through selling more of the UK's best services and goods overseas. Alongside this, there would be an additional benefit for everyone: cheaper imported goods improve everybody's standard of living.

So from the 1980s a series of international agreements began to reduce international trade barriers. The volume of goods traded internationally was transformed. Prior to the 1980s, for example, little coal was imported into the UK. Now, in contrast, imported coal is the predominant source and the last of the UK's deep coal mines has closed. Even the UK's most efficient underground mines were uncompetitive compared with lower-unit-cost countries, particularly where they were cutting coal using opencast mining methods.

The coal industry wasn't unique. The price of many UK traded goods has fallen back in real terms[2] over the last 30 years, while lots of premium jobs have driven up UK wages. For instance, not only has the absolute price of clothing and footwear progressively fallen,[3] but alongside this many of us have enjoyed the ability to buy more as our wages have increased. Indeed, the relatively open nature of the UK economy, with abundant competition on the high street and the growth of the internet, has meant that the decline in clothing costs in this country has been even greater than in France or the US.[4] The UK has – until recently – embraced globalisation more fully than most, and therefore felt the effects more strongly.

Given the severity of this increased competition, the UK's indigenous clothing industry, shoemakers and ceramics producers have all suffered industrial casualties – along with many others. Like the deep coal mines, many domestic producers found their local manufacturing operations became unviable. Over the last three decades, many closed their UK factories and transferred production to territories in the developing world with lower unit costs.

---

2   In real terms: adjusted to take account of UK inflation.

3   Real clothing and footwear prices in sterling terms. *Consumer Prices in the UK: Explaining the decline in real consumer prices for cars and clothing and footwear.* March 2015. Cambridge Econometrics.

4   March 2015. Cambridge Econometrics.

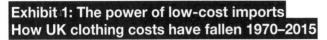

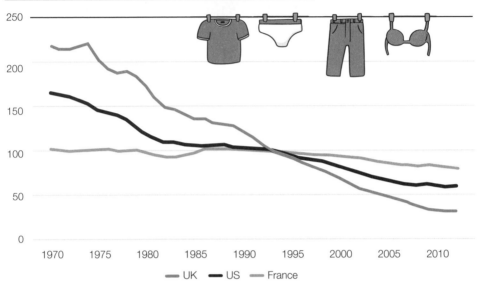

Exhibit 1: The power of low-cost imports
How UK clothing costs have fallen 1970–2015

March 2015. Source: Cambridge Econometrics

Although UK manufacturing jobs might have been lost, there has indeed been lots of employment generated elsewhere. Jobs have been created in areas where the UK has world-leading expertise – many areas of technological strength, for instance, have enjoyed premium growth. The pharmaceutical industry is a good example; it has been a major beneficiary of the opening up of international markets. Over recent decades, this sector has expanded as newer drugs have been developed and the commercial returns on these new medicines have been greatly improved through extra volumes sold at high margins throughout world markets.

There has been expansion elsewhere too. The media sector has enjoyed plenty of growth. It is not only the BBC that has increased its overseas sales significantly. Completely new industry sectors have been established and become sizeable too – the UK has become one of the leading centres for video games development, for example, with operations springing up in different areas, including Leamington Spa, Guildford, Cambridge, Dundee, as well as London.

The bottom line is that the last great social and political change in the UK created the economic reality of Great Britain as we currently know it. Globalisation boosted UK growth, and this persisted in the longest period of uninterrupted growth in modern times.

This underlines just how much social and political change is interrelated with longer-term economic and market trends. The outlook for a modern economy is defined by factors like these. But now social attitudes are hardening against globalisation, and this will have profound implications for the UK's financial future – the former status quo is already past its peak.

Credit, credit, credit

Indeed, the implications are particularly profound because of one key economic area that changed as part of the wave of social and political transformation. Alongside growth in international trade, there was an important parallel in the increasing availability of credit. This took place after debt markets were deregulated from the mid-1980s. The effects of this change have taken on a life of their own.

Usually extra growth from the deregulation of debt markets would have led to rising inflationary pressures. Normally, the rising inflationary impact of the extra growth would have been choked off through a series of consequential interest rates rises. **However, over the last three decades, the inflationary pressures from the deregulation of the debt markets were matched by an element of deflation introduced by the growth of international trade.**

So despite a growing willingness to take on credit, and the relatively rapid growth of the UK economy, the official rate of inflation defied critics and tended to moderate. UK interest rates have progressively declined over the decades, making it cheaper and cheaper for those in debt.

This was the great credit boom.

It wasn't all plain sailing, of course. There were economic wobbles along the way. UK interest rates were forced up to 10% when the government sought to keep the sterling exchange rate high enough to shadow the European Exchange Rate Mechanism (a forerunner of the euro).[5] In a final desperate move, the government even moved the UK interest rate up to 12%, and then 15% in a single day, to try to keep the value of sterling within an agreed band. But once it realised it could not sustain the exchange rate of sterling within agreed limits, a devaluation and reduction in the interest rate meant the UK went on to enjoy its longest period of uninterrupted economic growth in modern times.[6]

It is important to recognise that this period of massive credit growth was most unusual. Liberalising trade and deregulating the debt and financial markets changed the UK's economic trajectory in a major way. And given that most other developed economies were following the same change simultaneously, it was a trend reflected in nearly all developed markets together. But ultimately a credit boom can only ever be just a phase – it merely happened to be a phase that lasted for decades. And, as we are now seeing socially and politically, globalisation itself now appears to be in remission.

What the financial world will look like when globalisation and the credit boom draw to a close is a question of vital importance for investors, and others too. In order to address this ultimate question, we must first look in more detail at exactly how globalisation and the credit boom have been reflected in financial market trends. It makes for an interesting and somewhat unexpected story:

• **Chapter two** sets out the vast growth of the financial industry in the UK alongside one of the key drivers of corporate growth over the past 30 years.

---

5   European Exchange Rate Mechanism (ERM): Prior to the introduction of the euro the currencies of member states of the planned currency union were semi-pegged, fixed within bands, in an attempt to reduce variability in exchange rates and promote stability.

6   Between 1993 and 2003 UK GDP increased without any incidences of two successive negative quarters, technically regarded as signaling a recession.

- **Chapter three** links these changes with corporate culture – and, despite the lessons of the Global Financial Crisis, shows how imprudence has arguably become more engrained since 2008.

- **Chapter four** draws attention to a second credit boom of extraordinary intensity and all its associated dangers.

- **Chapter five** discusses how the long period of growth has unbalanced the corporate mix between the mature and the vibrant.

- **Chapter six** covers the risk that UK corporate profit margins are in the process of peaking out – and the challenges that will present in the future.

- **Chapter seven** highlights how investment strategies might change as the previous economic and market trends come to an end as globalisation retreats.

The second half of the book considers how investors can respond as these distortions unwind, and markets get used to an economy with a more natural rhythm of growth and decay:

- **Chapter eight** asks whether it is time for the most significant shift in asset allocation for decades. It discusses why it will be vital for investors to actively select those companies that are vibrant and vigorous. Investors will also have a renewed opportunity to be socially useful, because the best stocks will be those driving extra job creation, tax take and wage growth as well as portfolio returns.

- **Chapter nine** explores the first of several factors that define a truly vibrant and attractive investment prospect in the economic future: companies with niches (but not just any old company or any old niche).

- **Chapter ten** reviews a more wide-ranging factor for the future: how to access productivity improvement and in doing so contribute to driving up the efficiency of the wider economy.

- **Chapter eleven** examines how companies offering superior service can sustain attractive margins.

- **Chapter twelve** covers three ways to minimise risk within what will be a smaller universe of premium stocks in future, given that there won't be an ocean of liquidity to stave off recessions and corporate failure.

Lastly, in the **Conclusion**, I summarise how the face of finance will change as globalisation pulls back from its high-water mark.

CHAPTER TWO:

The Strange Case of Corporate Profits

One of the features of the credit boom that has attracted relatively little comment is the scale of corporate margin improvement over recent decades.

Stellar growth

The latest phase of globalisation, which began in earnest in the mid-1980s, was an extraordinary period for most businesses. Many expanded in scale for years, enjoying an extended period of supernormal sales and profit growth. Over a 30-year period, the aggregate value of large, mainstream companies listed on the UK stock market surged – rising from £165 billion in 1985 to over £1.6 trillion by 2015.[7] If the dividend income paid out on these shares is included, the rise in aggregate value over the period is over 14-fold.

---

7   Market capitalisation of companies listed in the FTSE 100, based on valuations at 31 December 1985 and 31 December 2015. Source: FTSE Russell.

The gigantic scale of this stock market appreciation over that 30-year period is principally down to a number of positive trends coming through together:

- The globalisation of world trade drove corporate sales growth at an unusually fast rate for decades.

- Debt tends to be a cheaper (although riskier) way to fund corporate growth. The deregulation of the credit markets enhanced growth, too, as debt could be used to fund additional corporate expansion. As interest rates fell, this boosted the profitability of those using debt even further.

- The valuations of equities are heavily determined by the level of long-term bond yields. So the extraordinary reduction in long-term bond yields over the last three decades greatly enhanced the valuation of corporate earnings.

- The final factor is the sheer length of time that these favourable factors have been sustained.

It is the combination of a strong and ongoing rise in profitability, along with rising valuations on those earnings, that has driven the extraordinary appreciation of equity markets. And when a strongly positive trend is sustained for decades, the overall scale of absolute gains can be spectacular.

Exhibit 2: Notional drivers of the substantial rise in equity prices

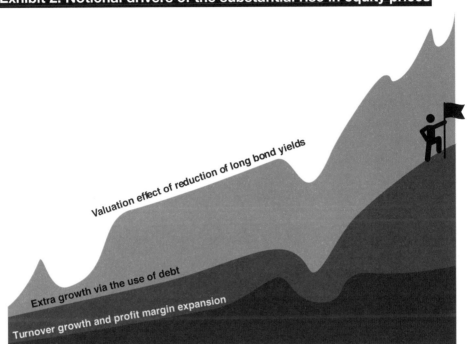

Valuation effect of reduction of long bond yields

Extra growth via the use of debt

Turnover growth and profit margin expansion

1992   1996   2000   2004   2008   2012   2016

The financial services industry enjoyed exceptional growth as both stock markets and the trading of corporate credit boomed. The financial services sector in the UK is more international than most others, so the combination of the growth of the sector, and the globalisation of its operations, came together with the City becoming one of the most successful areas of business in the UK.

In my first book – *Slow Finance* – I outlined just how much the culture of the financial sector had changed over three decades from 1980. Globalisation might have greatly enhanced the growth of the media and the pharmaceutical sectors, but the same trend had an even more extreme effect on the City.

As the global debt markets scaled up, the traded debt markets have grown to dwarf the core UK equity markets. Innovations came through too (typical of boom periods): the UK financial sector embraced sophisticated financial derivatives. Traded options, structured products, collateralised debt obligations, asset-backed mortgages – all became sizeable markets.

The financial services industry is now simply enormous, with some US$2,000 billion of foreign exchange traded through London every day.[8] *Slow Finance* highlighted how the huge scaling up in the financial sector had contributed to the financial sector becoming oversized in comparison to the rest of the UK economy.

Exhibit 3: Surging capital flows

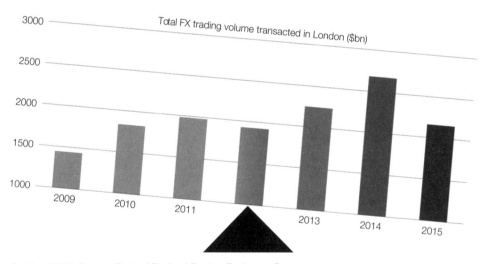

October 2015. Source: Bank of England Foreign Exchange Survey

---

8   Bank of England Foreign Exchange Survey 2015. Source: Bloomberg.

Defying gravity

There have been plenty of corporate profits along the way. Profit share[9] within UK corporates rose to a peak around the dotcom boom at the start of 2000.[10] Since that time, profit margins have moderated somewhat, though they remain at elevated levels in most sectors.

Corporate profit share does tend to fluctuate over time. But the sustained rise in UK corporate profitability raises a significant and uncomfortable question. **Why have our profit margins risen so far, given that any increase would normally be expected to be transitory?**

After all, if a particular area of economic activity generates premium returns, theory suggests that it will attract new capital and the extra competition will normally compete away the elevated margin. Yet corporate profit margins have not only remained elevated – they have done so for a long period of time.

One way to attempt to explain this phenomenon is to compare the UK's experience with that of other economies over recent decades. Exhibit 4 outlines how US corporate profit share has changed since 1985.[11] US profit share used to average around 7% of GDP in the 1980s. The ratio jumped to close to 10% by the mid-1990s as the world credit boom became established. While profit share did track back for a while thereafter, it ultimately surged again, reaching around 12% ahead of the Global Financial Crisis in 2008. In spite of a severe economic setback over 2009, this ratio subsequently fully recovered and remains elevated at around the 11% mark.

Although US and UK trends are not identical, the sizeable rise and sustained increase in US profit margins since the 1980s is similar across both territories.

---

9   The percentage of corporate turnover allocated to profit. This is not the same as the percentage of corporate profits expressed as a percentage of GDP, as it is calculated prior to the deduction of tax charges.

10   Andrew Hunt Economics.

11   US corporate profits adjusted for inventory valuation and capital consumption, expressed as a percentage of GDP. The adjustments reflect the way in which the valuations of inputs, e.g. energy costs and inventory, may fluctuate over time. As at September 2015. Source: Andrew Hunt Economics.

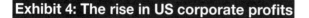

Exhibit 4: The rise in US corporate profits

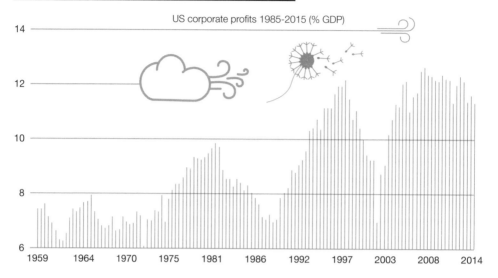

US corporate profits 1985-2015 (% GDP)

September 2015. Source: Andrew Hunt Economics

It might be tempting to equate this general improvement in corporate margins with technological innovation. Aside from word processing, computers were barely used within businesses prior to 1985, whereas most companies now embrace technology as a central part of their operations. However, this explanation doesn't really stand up to detailed consideration.

Take the car industry as an example. Car manufacturers have fully embraced technological change and most have greatly improved their productivity over the last three decades. The performance of modern cars is now vastly superior compared with models released 30 years ago – yet the profit margin on most volume car brands has not much improved. Sales of many Western brands might have grown during the credit boom, but so too has the intensity of competition. In fact, the reduction in trade barriers has added to the number of competing brands in most developed economies. So whilst there are plenty of customers still willing to buy luxury cars with lots of extras, there are still plenty of other cars available at competitive import prices too.

Overall, the intensity of competition in the volume car market has increased and the efficiency gains that have come from embracing technology have only been transitory. If this was not the case, historic innovators like the shipping or railway industries would still be enjoying the premium margins associated with technological improvements that took place decades ago.

No – innovative improvements are only 'innovative' whilst the competition is catching up. Once other competitors are equally efficient, the extra profit margin attributable to the technological improvement is ceded.

So what explains such a sizeable and persistent rise in profitability across a whole economy like that of the US or the UK? In my view, the explanation for the sustained rise in corporate profit margins can only be the global credit boom. It is no coincidence that the timing of the initial improvement in margins coincided with the accelerating sales growth in the mid-1980s, just as the credit boom gained momentum.

Think of an economy in aggregate. In a simplified economy there are businesses providing services and products to the consumers within it. The businesses pay employees for their work, and all of the employees use this cash (plus the aggregated dividends from corporates) to pay for all the goods and services that they buy. However, if consumers collectively borrow a little extra cash to buy extra goods, the borrowed cash inflates the turnover of the businesses a little faster than their costs.

Of course, there are additional wages needed to fund the extra production of goods and services, but the scale of the extra revenues usually exceeds the scale of the extra costs. For example, the more intensive use of assets like a manufacturing plant or office space will not tend to add as much extra cost as the associated growth in revenues.

In this simplified model, **a general rise in consumer borrowing boosts sales faster than costs**. So the bottom line is that corporate profit margins do indeed tend to rise during credit booms.

This can be expressed another way. *Corporate profit margins can be expected to move inversely with changes in the savings ratio.* A glance at the trend in the UK savings ratio does appear to have a similar – yet inverted – pattern to the general and sustained rise in corporate profit margins:

Exhibit 5: The slump in UK households' savings ratio

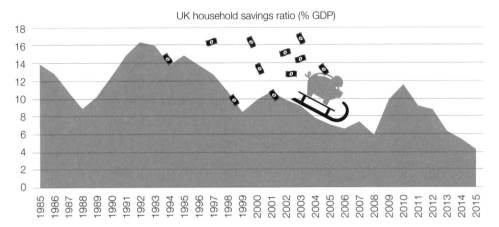

UK household savings ratio (% GDP)

April 2016. Source: UK Office for National Statistics

Since the mid-1980s, the inclination to borrow has become more widespread and the UK savings ratio has greatly reduced. Generally, UK consumers have saved less and become more willing to borrow, and this has driven extra growth in corporate sales. Similarly, as companies have funded extra growth through taking on more debt, there have been inevitable spillover effects elsewhere. The surge in expenditure has contributed to a period of unusually vibrant economic growth during the credit boom. The credit boom has driven a major improvement in corporate profitability over the past three decades, and alongside this the increased willingness to take on debt has boosted a sustained rise in profit margins.

The implications are far-reaching and not entirely benign, as we will see in the next chapter.

CHAPTER THREE:

The Age of Plenty

The same pressures that have encouraged boards towards addressing internal areas of weakness have also pressurised boards to make decisions to improve the 'efficiency' of their balance sheets though using more debt.

Disappearing dual capital structures

The increase in corporate profit margins throughout the credit boom of the last 30 years has led to a pervasive and ongoing change of culture within corporate boards.

Prior to the credit boom, there was a perception that most of the UK's largest quoted companies were simply too large to be vulnerable to takeover. Smaller quoted companies didn't have that luxury, so they often minimised the risk of an unwelcome hostile approach by adopting a dual shareholding structure. Shareholder voting rights were concentrated among a limited group of friendly Class A shareholders, while Class B shareholders enjoyed much of the commercial benefits of the growth of the business but lacked significant voting rights over corporate changes such as board appointments or hostile takeovers. Generally the price of Class A shares stood at a higher valuation as they came with the greater element of control.

It wasn't unusual for institutional investors to avoid investing in companies with dual capital structures given the perceived second-class nature of non-voting shares. Even so, prior to the credit boom the dual capital structure was a viable and commercial structure for many quoted businesses. But changes brought about by the credit boom undermined the advantages of the dual capital corporate structure.

The change with the greatest impact was the accelerated rise of asset prices during the last three decades. Easy access to extra capital gave people the ability to buy assets whose value was rising at an accelerated rate. **The real gunpowder, in terms of returns, comes from taking on extra debt alongside additional risk capital.**

The same effect was evident in the housing market. Those who were able to raise cash for a deposit on a second home were able to access extra debt in the form of an additional mortgage. And as house prices rose in value, the scale of the upside on that original cash deposit was often a multiple of its initial size. During the credit boom, the 'gearing' of assets enhanced the upside for those with access to additional capital, since in conjunction with the use of debt the extra returns could be very substantial.

The problem with dual share capital structures was that the lower share price made it more expensive to raise additional capital compared to those firms using ordinary share structures – after all, Class B shares naturally stand at a discount. And the fact that dual capital companies were often less popular with institutional investors tended to limit the sums that could be raised as well. So those with dual capital structures often missed out on their full potential to raise extra capital to participate in the credit boom. As this became apparent, most dual capital companies either proposed simplifying their capital structures to a uniform class of all ordinary shares, or else chose to delist from the exchange.

Takeovers and corporate culture

Alongside this, there was added interest in taking over other companies. Those companies that made acquisitions early in the credit boom typically went on to enjoy enhanced returns. The more this trend became established, the greater the number of investors who wanted to participate.

The same effect was again evident in the housing market. The longer house prices rose, the greater the investor interest. Gradually homeowners increased their participation from just one home to a second home – and over the last decade there was growing interest in buy-to-let homes as well.

In a similar manner, more and more corporate takeovers took place. Private equity entered the picture as well, frequently using much higher ratios of debt in its takeover funding structures. A confluence of all these factors contributed to an extraordinary rise in the volume and scale of merger and acquisition activity over the last three decades.

Exhibit 6: Global mergers and acquisitions

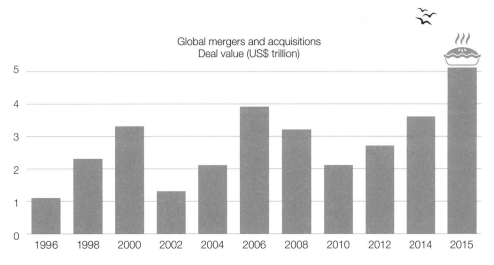

Global mergers and acquisitions
Deal value (US$ trillion)

Deal volume in US dollar terms. December 2015. Source: JP Morgan, Dealogic

The gradual disappearance of the protection associated with the dual capital structure, and the growing rate of takeover activity, has changed the culture of boards themselves:

- Lowly-geared companies, like houses without a mortgage, tend to make less money for the speculative investor. So the returns on quoted companies with little debt in their capital structures could be amplified simply by reducing the amount of risk equity in their capital structures and by swapping it with low-cost debt. Under-geared, slower-growth companies were therefore more liable to being picked off by others, especially as the amount of debt available became ever more plentiful.

- At a time of abundant growth, those firms that didn't fully participate tended to generate lower returns. Therefore quoted businesses that continued to keep corporate risks low – for example, through adopting slower growth strategies – also found themselves becoming vulnerable to takeover.

- Even the very largest firms came under this pressure in time. As the debt markets became more industrial in scale, it become plausible to fund takeovers of ever larger quoted companies.

Alongside this, the needs of the fund management sector changed. Prior to the credit boom, many fund managers ran portfolios investing in quoted companies that in aggregate were less risky than the markets overall. When there were regular recessions, clients naturally appreciated the value of this lower-risk attitude.

But during the credit boom, when returns on markets came through at higher levels, often for several years in a row, strategies that missed out on returns year after year became perceived as old-fashioned and out of touch. The longer the markets appreciated, the less fearful clients became of market setbacks. When annual returns are plentiful, any setbacks are quickly made up in following years. Client preferences evolved so that they became more attuned to measuring the effectiveness of their fund manager with reference to the performance of mainstream indices. This pressure to perform was then reflected by many fund managers themselves since they needed companies in their portfolios to embrace the dominant trends and fully participate in the boom.

Over time these factors drove nearly all quoted businesses to take part in the credit boom, even if this cranked up the levels of downside risk. In a dog-eat-dog world, it became much harder for any quoted company to propose anything out-of-line with a full participation in the boom. The rising rate of takeovers forced corporates to adopt more 'risk on' strategies.

So the very same pressures that encouraged the boards of quoted companies to unify their capital structures also ended up pressurising boards to adopt pro-cyclical attitudes to risk. The conversations were all about improving the 'efficiency' of corporate balance sheets – through striving for extra growth, often funded with extra debt as well as some additional equity.

Essentially those management teams that refused to adopt a speculative approach were gradually displaced by management teams with a much more speculative culture. This tended to magnify the market upside during the credit boom, even though it bred a culture of imprudence.

Pro-cyclical attitudes beyond 2008

Credit booms are wholly dependent upon an ever-increasing willingness to take on additional debt. In the same way that a pyramid scheme[12] is only sustainable whilst it is growing, eventually even a marginal setback in the willingness to issue or take on extra credit during a credit boom is enough to destabilise the whole.

By 2008, the global credit boom had grown old. Anything could have started the unwind at this point. Excessive lending to US subprime house purchasers proved to be the nexus of the setback, but if it hadn't been that, another factor would have been the trigger shortly thereafter.

---

12   A pyramid scheme: an investment scheme where returns are generated from new capital contributions from other investors rather than productive investment. The structure is only sustainable as long as the flow of capital from new investors is sustained.

The sheer scale of the Global Financial Crisis in 2008 underlined just how much risk had accumulated over prior decades. The duration and magnitude of the credit boom had become so vast that its sudden peaking out endangered the viability of the entire capitalist system, with the banks being the worst affected.

Since 2008 the collective aim of politicians and regulators has been to ensure that banks unwind this imprudent risk-taking. They have sought to reduce systemic risk through raising their capital ratios, so that banks are more prudently financed and less vulnerable to major setbacks. A rising safety margin on their capital reserves covering their loan books[13] makes it more costly for banks to fund debt. Banks in developed markets have therefore scaled back their activities and refocused on those areas where they have material commercial advantages. Nearly every major Western bank has downsized its operations since 2008. Alongside this, there has been a major change in their internal cultures too.

But there were risks of going 'cold turkey' on the supply of debt. Central banks were careful to ensure that debt markets did not freeze up entirely, since this would almost certainly have led to an economic depression. The aim has been to unwind the worst excesses of the credit boom gradually. So once interest rates were reduced to 'emergency' levels in developed markets, they have remained at these levels given that world growth has not grown out of control. Quantitative easing (QE)[14] has been introduced as well. This has had the effect of reducing the long-term cost of debt and has made it easier for corporates and mortgages to be funded. Both of these policies saved many corporates from going bust during the 2008 setback and contributed to their considerable recovery subsequently. Most companies have been able to extend the term of their debts as necessary, while also benefitting from lower ongoing interest costs.

---

13   Prudential Regulation Authority. *The capital adequacy of banks: Today's issue and what we have learnt from the past.* Andrew Bailey. 10 July 2014.

14   Quantitative easing involves the electronic creation of money by central banks, which is used to improve the flow of money in the economy through asset purchases and by indirectly reducing borrowing costs.

But the policy of keeping interest rates 'lower for longer' has obscured the fact that an imprudent culture had built up within other parts of the corporate sector during the credit boom. Corporate debt has come to be seen as something that can be taken on for the very long term – it does not cost much and can be refinanced as necessary. With interest rates still low, this view has remained unchanged: renewed prudence within the banking sector has not come through elsewhere.

The pro-cyclical culture that dominated many corporate and fund management teams has generally remained in place *following* the Global Financial Crisis. The extraordinary returns on equity markets subsequent to 2009 have if anything seemed to reinforce the justification of the previous stance.

All this would be worrying enough – but the developed world is not the only part of the global economy facing the unintended consequences of too much debt, as discussed in the next chapter.

CHAPTER FOUR:

The Second Major Credit Boom

The expansionary phase of the Chinese credit boom has made it easier for regulators to let the heat out of the global credit boom, but it has further deferred the stimulus for a change of culture within financial markets.

Boom boom

Naturally there is an inclination to avoid making the same mistake twice, especially in a relatively short time frame. So the severe existential risks that became so worrying at the end of the credit boom have been something that most central banks have sought to avoid repeating. As long as the severe setback remains in mind, our politicians and central banks will work against allowing banks to make the same mistake again. For now this has involved introducing extra regulations and increased capital ratios for the banks, with an aim of making it nearly impossible for them to take such extreme risks in future.

And yet there has been a *second* credit boom developing elsewhere. Despite our recent problems with excessive leverage, away from developed economies another credit boom has been building – and not slowly.

The Chinese economy was the prime beneficiary of the globalisation of world trade over recent decades. The reduction of international trade barriers was hugely beneficial and the Chinese authorities put together a set of policies that allowed the country to grow its aggregate employment incredibly fast by taking a disproportionate market share of the globalisation of trade.

Exhibit 7: China's growing share of world trade

China's growing share of world trade (%)

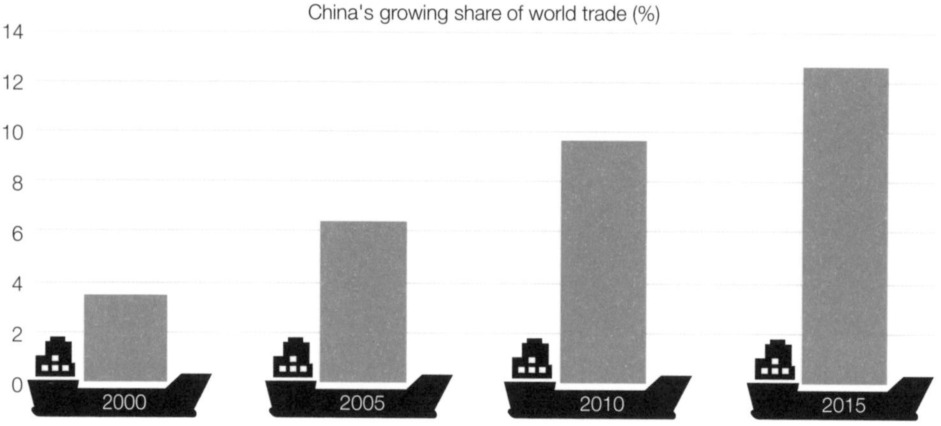

May 2016. Source: Andrew Hunt Economics

Importantly, prior to 2008 much of the growth of the Chinese economy was funded by capital from overseas investors. Therefore Chinese banks were not caught out by excessive leverage in 2008. The Chinese banking system did not have a banking crisis at that time. Excessive bank leverage in developed economies was perceived by the Chinese authorities as a fault of Western governments, who operated with insufficient central planning.

In contrast to other countries, China didn't need any economic retrenchment after 2008. China's main problem was the step back in world growth and its impact on the country's ongoing plans to sustain rapid growth of Chinese employment. One way to bridge this problem was to accelerate investment in infrastructure. This would meet the Chinese authorities' principal policy objective of creating further new employment at a time when the worst of the global downturn was coming through.[15] The thinking was that the new infrastructure would also put China in an even better position to grow employment thereafter, through taking additional market share in the next phase of global growth.

The step-up in infrastructure spend was led by Chinese local authorities. But they had little access to risk capital, so most used dedicated new structures to borrow from local banks[16], which helped fund new developments. Alongside this, preferential financing arrangements were put in place for China's numerous state-owned companies. Many also bought land and property on a speculative basis.

With both the state and private sector investing, the infrastructure boom quickly took on a momentum of its own. For several years, local authorities sold new flats for windfall profits and this facilitated yet faster housing construction. Using debt as fuel, growth in Chinese infrastructure expenditure accelerated, with local authorities planning on an ever larger scale – ultimately even setting their sights on brand new cities with new transport links and airports.

---

15   *China's stimulus package.* Economist, 12 November 2008.

16   *China's Big Bang.* Thomson Reuters, November 2010.

A helping hand

This was a magnificent period for Chinese growth, especially in comparison with that of the rest of the world. In fact, **China's infrastructure investment, driven by borrowing and spending, is thought to have generated around one third of the world's entire growth in the seven years following the Global Financial Crisis.**[17]

It is worth reflecting on this for a moment – had the Chinese economy flatlined after 2008, the financial consequences of the Global Financial Crisis would have been much more severe within developed economies. The acceleration of Chinese growth came at a very useful time for developed countries' central banks. Their unusually aggressive policies of QE and super-low interest rates were all the more effective because they were harnessed to extra growth from China, and together they prompted a global recovery that was much better than expected.

In addition, the Chinese infrastructure boom accelerated demand for commodities, so there was a major recovery in the prices of oil, copper and iron ore. Since many of these originated from emerging economies, those countries found that they were also jolted back into growth after 2008. It almost appeared that emerging economies had magically 'decoupled' from the economic problems of developed markets. So capital allocators also funded the growth of emerging markets after 2008, fuelling the momentum.

However, it should be remembered that this period of world growth was largely built on the Chinese infrastructure boom. And by 2015 the Chinese economy was funding nearly one quarter of all capital expenditure in the world.

---

17   *China: Size matters.* iMFdirect, 26
     March 2016.

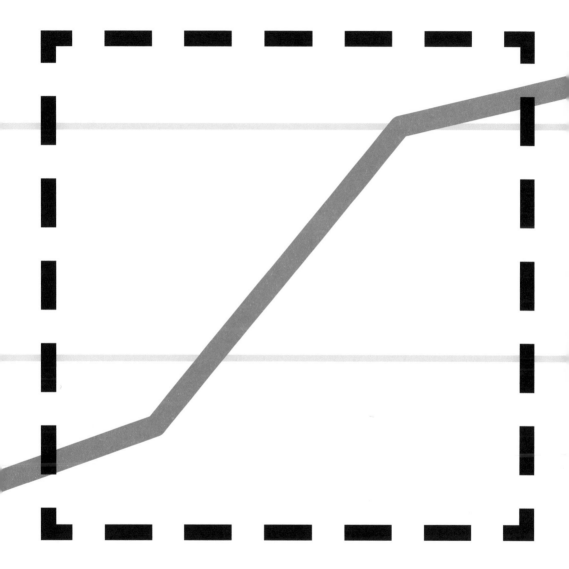

Exhibit 8: Chinese capital expenditure
Investment as a percentage of global investment, 1985–2015

2016. Source: Credit Suisse Global Equity Strategy 2016 Outlook: Themes, Sectors and Styles

Unintended consequences

There are drawbacks to such a rapid increase in capital expenditure, especially given its foundation on a narrow geography and a limited range of industry sectors. It tends to come with an increased risk of capital misallocation.

Initially the extra infrastructure spend was directed at those areas where there were known needs for improvement. But as these bottlenecks were resolved, funding moved on to more marginal projects. Over time, the gigantic growth in infrastructure spend led to overbuild, with real questions over whether the momentum of spend was more significant than its appropriateness.

The key point is that infrastructure investment on this scale, over many years, ultimately becomes less and less productive for an economy going forward. For example, the huge rise in Chinese house prices encouraged far too much state overbuild, to the extent that more than one in five urban homes in China stood empty in 2013.[18] Elsewhere, the huge growth in infrastructure spend led to far too much capacity within suppliers as well. As a result the Chinese economy has been left with hideous overcapacity within the steel and cement industries.

As these excesses and imbalances became more obvious, they spilled over with Chinese house prices peaking. As this came into view, the rate of new housebuilding started decelerating from the end of 2012 – the price of copper was one of the first commodities to reflect the change in trend. By 2014 the absolute market values in the Chinese property market had begun to fall sharply,[19] with the Chinese stock market experiencing a major selloff in the middle of 2015.[20]

The reversal of commodity prices quickly changed the dynamics of many emerging market economies. The unexpected reversal of investment fundamentals provoked an outflow of overseas capital. When combined with falling commodity revenues,

---

18 *Survey and Research Center for China Household Finance.* Southwestern University of Finance and Economics, China, 2014.

19 *China home price drop spreads as housing demand weakens.* Bloomberg, 18 September 2014.

20 *China share plunge smacks world markets.* Reuters, 24 August 2015.

the currencies of most emerging economies weakened considerably. Most were forced to keep their interest rates at high-ish levels to slow the devaluation of their currencies, irrespective of the adverse effect this had on their economic slowdown. There was little governments could do to soften the downturn.

Perhaps one of the most extreme economic setbacks came in Brazil. The exchange rate of the Brazilian real versus the US dollar approximately halved over 2014–16, and interest rates had to stay around 14% to prevent the currency falling further. The Brazilian government sought to soften the risk of a recession by running up its budget deficit to well over 10% of GDP,[21] even though this is a position that is hopelessly unsustainable for more than a few quarters. However, despite these policies aimed at softening the economic setback, Brazil has been caught in a recession that is probably the worst it has seen since the 1930s.

Brazil is not unique. Most emerging economies have been caught out by the setback in commodity prices, with growth in developed economies being sub-normal in most cases as well. Perhaps we shouldn't be surprised that the oil price eventually fell by around two thirds between the middle of 2014 and the early part of 2016.

The combination of a world slowdown and a loss of growth momentum in China brought things to a head for the Chinese authorities. By the middle of 2015 there was a real danger that Chinese unemployment would start to rise. The position was even more difficult to manage because Chinese banks were on the brink of suffering a domestic credit crunch.

The Chinese opted to embrace the credit boom yet more closely.

Debt was injected into the economy at an even faster rate. Fighting the end of a credit boom with extra debt cannot work for very long, but may keep employment growing for a little bit longer. The key question is whether a credit boom of this magnitude can ever be unwound in a well-ordered manner.

---

21 Brazil's budget deficit reached a record level in 2015, equivalent to 10.3% of GDP. Source: Bloomberg.

One big bubble

It is estimated that Chinese debt grew more than tenfold in the decade ending in 2015.[22] Since 2008, total debt within the Chinese economy has increased at almost twice the pace it did in the UK and US in the years running up to the 2008 setback, with the profile of debt accelerating through the period.[23] **In the year to June 2016 it was estimated that Chinese policymakers had created debt amounting to approximately 40% of the Chinese economy in an attempt to sustain its positive momentum.** These are simply giant sums by any measure – all the more so given the global scale of the Chinese economy and the short time frame in which the debt was created.

In fact, the debt boom has been growing so fast that it has been hard for Chinese banks to originate debt fast enough. The banks' reserve requirements have been steadily reduced to de-bottleneck the process. Economists now believe the scale of the Chinese credit boom to be amongst the largest ever witnessed[24] – larger than the UK bubble in the Lawson years in the 1980s, larger than the Japanese boom in the 1990s, and significantly larger than the US credit boom in the mid-2000s as well.[25]

---

22   Estimates from J Kylie Bass at Hayman Capital Management suggest that China's banking assets grew from under US$3 trillion to over US$34.5 trn.

23   Luigi Buttiglione, Philip Lane, Lucrezia Reichlin and Vincent Reinhart. *Deleveraging, what deleveraging? Total debt, excluding financials, expressed as a percentage of GDP*. International Center for Monetary and Banking Studies, 2014.

24   Credit excesses – and busts – that we have known. Andrew Hunt Economics, 13 May 2016.

25   It is interesting to note that while the extra credit created by China has helped corporate margins expand in the developed world, it has not had the same impact in China. The inefficient allocation of capital, especially alongside the principal aim of generating employment instead of profit, and the inclination of Chinese nationals to save given there is almost no social security and national healthcare, has resulted in their corporate profit share being remarkably low.

$7tn
2007

$28tn
2014

2015. McKinsey Global Institute. Debt (and not much) deleveraging

Remember too that most Chinese state-owned entities are not run on commercial grounds. Most are only marginally profitable, with many routinely operating at a loss. The fact that many are now heavily indebted means that most firms have no real chance of ever generating enough cash to meet formal debt-repayment schedules.[26] For now, all that can be done is to roll over the loans as they become due in the hope that things may get a little better in future.

The Chinese credit boom might have played an important role in moderating the unwinding of some of the credit excesses within developed economies after 2008. However, with the rapid growth of the Chinese economy now falling away, the slowdown in world growth is the dominant trend going forward. We can no longer expect the economic norms of the credit boom to return. Instead there is a greater risk of 'stop/go' economic cycles, characterised by periods of modest growth interspersed with recessions.

* * *

Let's review the main issues so far. Three decades ago a change in our collective social and political attitudes ushered in a period of exceptional growth, driven by the globalisation of trade and the deregulation of credit. Whilst this has come through in extra returns for investors, more employment, better tax take for governments, and a wide-ranging reduction in the cost of consumer goods, there have been drawbacks. Globalisation also introduced:

- returns that have been so consistently good that the incautious have been disproportionally rewarded over the prudent

- the need for unprecedented actions from central banks across the developed world to prevent a world depression when the credit boom peaked

- ultra-low interest rates and QE since 2008, which have contributed to yet more complacency in many industries – except (ironically) in banking

---

26   Credit Suisse Global Equity Strategy. 2016 Outlook: Themes, Sectors and Styles.

- a second credit boom, to offset the aftermath of the Global Financial Crisis, this time in China – a national boom, but an extraordinarily intense boom nonetheless.

In other words, globalisation has come with both positives and negatives. Over the last 30 years, the positives have often been predominant. But as globalisation peaks, some of the negatives are coming into view, and these are prompting social attitudes to change once again.

Globalisation is now in retreat, and this will introduce a long period when the prudent will be rewarded over the incautious. The next chapter highlights the nature of some of the vulnerabilities that have become incumbent during the booms.

CHAPTER FIVE:

The Balance Between Growth and Decay

Beyond 2008, corporate productivity has stagnated and impeded our ability to fund increasing tax take for governments and ongoing wage improvement.

Growth and decay

The world of global trade and credit is all tied together in an international ecosystem. Indeed, the business sector can be likened to a forest. During a boom, there are plenty of good ingredients for growth, just as within a forest there's plenty of soil, water and warm sunshine. When the weather is favourable, there's plenty of growth. Overall, forests are good for plant growth, and expanding economies are good for corporate growth. With easy access to both risk capital and debt, and a growing global marketplace, the UK economy has enjoyed a long period of expansion over the last 30 years.

Large trees thrive in forests because of the elevated nature of the leaf canopy. The largest have extensive root systems that can tap plenty of nutrients and water, but crucially they also have scope to reach up to the sunshine. In contrast, smaller plants are mostly overshadowed. They may have nutrients and water, but few of those on the forest floor have much access to direct sunlight.

Natural woodland and forests are stable ecosystems because they have a good balance of growth and decay. Growth is facilitated by decay because it liberates nutrients for the more vigorous to reuse. Growth and decay come together in a balanced mix of maturity and vitality. As the largest trees age, they eventually rot after their vitality ebbs away. In time, the collapse of ancient trees starts the process of bringing through the more vigorous by releasing nutrients for subsequent generations. Even more importantly, gaps created in the canopy allow light to reach the less mature, helping some of the most vibrant to enjoy a period of unusually rapid growth.

The importance of the concept of a balance between growth and decay isn't new. Georg Hegel, the 18th century philosopher, was one of the first to write extensively about the tension between the two. He championed the term 'sublation', a term that encompassed the apparently contradictory forces of change and preservation together. Regular readers of economics texts will also be aware of the term 'Schumpeter's wind'. Joseph Schumpeter, an Austrian economist who worked in the 1930s, was particularly interested in the balance between economic growth and its dependence on economic destruction to succeed. He coined the term 'creative destruction' to explain how something as negative as decay was absolutely central to ensuring economies retained the opportunity to grow.

Growth and decay in the financial sector

The problem with the financial world is that the mix of growth and decay is rarely as well-balanced as that of a forest. During periods of economic growth, markets tend to cull too few of the moribund. At the end of sustained periods of growth, the well-established and mature are typically overly represented. And being aged, many of the mature are not especially vibrant or efficient. They remain perfectly viable whilst conditions are good, since they have the advantage of being an incumbent. But when conditions turn down, the over-borrowed tend to lose out and quite a number of corporates risk failure. So during setbacks, the economic pendulum often over-swings to a surfeit of decay, and the economy pitches into a recession.

The cycle then stabilises and reverses, because the extra decay opens up more opportunity for the vigorous and the overshadowed. Those with greater vitality are able to take advantage of the voids vacated by the casualties. The economic pendulum swings once again towards a period of more general growth.

The financial world tends to act more like a temperate woodland than, say, a rainforest. Periods of growth are followed by periods of more wide-ranging decay, which can be likened to corporate summers and winters.

Booms and busts

Just occasionally extraneous factors undermine the normal seasonal pattern and the financial forest remains fixed in growth mode for an extended period. Without regular winters, growth and decay move more and more out of balance. During booms, with few corporate failures, the tall and the incumbent dominate for even longer, with the accumulated scale and tenure of the mainstream frustrating the expansionary potential of the vigorous and immature.

The globalisation of trade and the deregulation of financial markets created an economic boom that persisted for a good three decades after Big Bang in 1986. This exceptional period of growth might have enhanced corporate growth and stock market returns for many years – but it came at the expense of too little corporate decay. And without any real economic setbacks,[27] many corporations became more and more overextended and inefficient – after all, even marginal operations generated a return.

Such long-terms booms bring about a huge challenge when the trend peaks out. After a boom, an unusually large corps of corporates is vulnerable. Well-established

---

27   The UK stock market setback from 2000 to 2003 was not a real economic setback as the UK economy didn't suffer a pronounced recession in the period. Most 'old economy' mainstream stocks continued to trade successfully through this period.

companies within the canopy can carry considerable inefficiencies whilst conditions are benign. But when economic conditions become more challenging, the complex nature of their businesses and their inability to flex with change sets them at a considerable disadvantage – putting them at greater risk of failure.

All this leads to a major problem at the end of boom phases. Cutbacks amongst a vast number of companies simultaneously not only leads to an inevitable economic bust, but also tends to precipitate huge social distress as well. At the end of booms, the economic pendulum is prone to over-swing more than unusual, with a corporate cull that can be crippling for an economy. Companies in the fastest-growing sectors often turn out to be the most vulnerable when the setback arrives.

A good example is the Royal Bank of Scotland plc, which grew its assets to be worth an estimated £2.2 trillion in 2008, via rapid growth and a series of takeovers. The company's balance sheet eventually amounted to a value that surpassed the entire gross domestic product of the UK and Spain combined.[28] And like most other mainstream banks, RBS then found it was a vast and hopelessly overstretched organisation when the setback arrived. When the boom did peak in the form of the Global Financial Crisis, RBS was a very large and dangerously unstable business that could only avoid failure by calling upon massive government support.

Significantly, the overextended nature of the banking sector has prompted a period of huge retrenchment. Most have been obliged to cut back their range of operations to those where each perceives it has a genuine commercial advantage. The really interesting fact is that the cutbacks in most mainstream banks have opened up room in their non-core markets for a newer collection of more agile and vigorous lenders to come through. Some eight years after the crisis, the UK banking sector is now characterised by a much better mix of both the mature and the immature.

Perhaps even more importantly, it is a sector that is marked by renewed corporate vitality, with an aspiring collection of immature lenders and fintechs,[29] along with

---

28   Gore, G. *The fall and (partial) rise of RBS. IFR Review of the Year 2012*. Source: International Financing Review.

29   Fintechs: businesses in the financial sector that are taking advantage of computer technologies to deliver their services often in a novel and more efficient manner.

a series of larger financial groups, building societies and banks. And this more balanced ecosystem can be expected to be much more resilient should there be another crisis in the future.

Suppressing growth in corporate cash flow

Our collective problem is that following 2008 very few other industrial sectors entered a period of corporate decay. As in Schumpeter's thesis of creative destruction, the lack of decay ultimately ends up limiting growth. If the unproductive are artificially propped up, those with greater growth and vigour are consistently denied their opportunity to come through.

And the longer that decay is inhibited, the more the underlying vigour and productivity within the economy runs down as a number of the stagnant incumbents remain in place. In time, if this stultification becomes wide-ranging and deeply entrenched across an economy, it is expressed in economic stagnation.

Nearly three decades ago, when Japan faced the end of its major economic boom, the authorities initially let Darwinian forces take their course. However, the sheer scale of the corporate decay was so severe that the social consequences quickly became intolerable. Therefore the government and central bank were forced to introduce a number of emergency stimuli that arrested the natural process of decay, in the hope of having a more controlled period of corporate rebalancing instead. The aggressive reduction of interest rates and the implementation of QE[30] were equivalent to introducing a burst of artificial stimulus into the economic forest.

But with the benefit of hindsight, the Japanese policy of permanent stimulus has gradually fallen into an unhealthy new equilibrium. The ongoing use of ultra-low interest rates and QE may have electoral advantages because an ongoing recession doesn't win many votes. But keeping corporate failure sub-normal also continues to frustrate those with greater vigour – firms that would flourish should any new

---

30   Some wonder how a term like 'quantitative' could ever come to become part of the English lexicon. Quantitative is a translation of the Japanese word that described their process of QE decades before we came to it.

market opportunities open up. This situation has been in place for so long now that commentators' talk of Japan's economic 'lost decades'. The economy has reached the point of near standstill.

In the UK, the social consequences of a world depression after the 2008 Global Financial Crisis were far too severe to be tolerable, as in Japan. So governments and central banks resorted to the same policies, injecting additional stimulus every time there was a risk of a pick up in corporate decay. The repetition of the same policies makes them less and less effective each time. Gradually, there is a danger that we too will drift towards a future of lost decades and economic stagnation. The policies have unintentionally steered our business sector into a twilight world that is defined by a collective shortfall of capital expenditure. This is underlined by the complete lack of productivity improvement since 2008.

Japan failed to address problems for so long that when the more reform-minded Abe government finally took power, change was unwelcome and unwanted. By that point, the country's demographic headwinds were severe and the country had become conservative and moribund. As the West's demographics also begin to imply lower trend growth rates over the coming decades, we risk making the same mistake of leaving it too long.

The chart in exhibit 10 has important long-term implications. The absence of productivity improvement implies that corporate cash flow is no longer growing. And that has a direct impact on the ability to fund our ongoing social agenda. It also undermines the returns for those saving for the future.

Exhibit 10: The slump in UK productivity
Whole economy labour productivity per hour

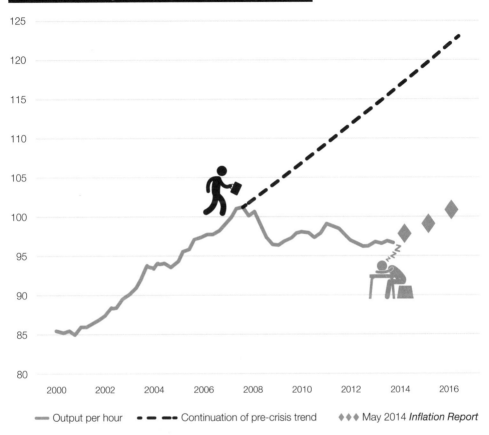

Legend: —— Output per hour   ● ━ ━● Continuation of pre-crisis trend   ◆◆◆ May 2014 *Inflation Report*

Pre-crisis trend growth is calculated between 1997 and Q1 2008, and is projected forward from Q1 2008. Source: Bank of England Quarterly Bulletin Q2 2014

The chart begs a series of important questions. Are developed economies like the UK condemned to becoming stagnant like Japan? Is the lack of corporate decay set to become a permanent feature? These questions are discussed in the context of additional headwinds up ahead in the next chapter.

CHAPTER SIX:

A Profits Recession

In my view, it is only a matter of when rather than if UK corporate profit share declines from here.

Planning for margin pressure

During the credit boom, economic growth progressed at a supernormal pace. Profit margins almost doubled too, so profits and corporate cash flow grew at an even faster pace. In chapter three the link was established between credit growth and the savings ratio. The chapter concluded that reductions in the UK household savings ratio were a key reason corporate profit margins had risen so significantly. Since 2008, the UK savings ratio has fallen even further, to a point where it has now reached lows that it hasn't touched since 1964.[31]

With little scope for further reductions in the saving ratio, there is no room for any improvement in UK profit margins. And in due course, profit margins will surely revert to the mean as the savings ratio returns to more normal levels. **All this implies that it is prudent for investors to plan on the basis that UK corporate profit margins will peak out and decline at some point in the future.**

31   UK Household savings ratio, as calculated by the UK Office for National Statistics. As at 31 December 2015.

In fact, profit margins in some sectors are already in decline. For example, the considerable reduction in commodity prices since 2014 has already slashed the profit margins of mineral extraction companies. If world growth continues at a much slower rate, the brutal truth is that commodity prices could be rebased at these lower levels for an extended period.

Whilst some companies do have market hedging in place, typically it extends for no more than a few years. So whilst this can be a great help in managing a period of change, commodity hedging does not actually arrest margin pressure – it just defers it. Commodity businesses might have to get used to operating at much lower profit margins.

Initially, markets were not unsettled by the collapse in commodity prices. Although the profitability of mining and oil companies was hit hard, it was assumed that there might be some offsetting benefits for those that consumed raw materials and energy. And many assumed that cheaper energy would be a new form of stimulus to boost the recovery of the world economy. So most assumed that corporate margins would not suffer overall. It was a case of swings and roundabouts – the winners and losers would broadly match each other. However, this rather upbeat analysis seems to have been confounded; US corporate profits peaked in January 2015 and have been on a broadly declining trajectory since that point.[32]

There are a number of reasons why the sharp reduction in commodity prices has impacted corporate margins in a wider range of stocks:

- Customers notice when commodity prices collapse. So although commodity consumers did indeed get an initial benefit from the reduced price of commodities, most have been obliged to pass these savings on to their customers via reduced pricing. And in time those customers have been obliged to pass their savings on to their customers too.

---

32   As at 26 August 2016. Includes preliminary estimate for Q2 2016. Source: US Bureau of Economics Analysis.

- Energy makes up a very large part of all global capital expenditure each year. It was estimated that some US$1,600 billion[33] was invested in the exploration and development of oil and gas reserves during 2013, so even minor cutbacks in spend can add up to a major reduction in capital investment. The abrupt setback in crude prices led to most oil companies shelving or cancelling projects that became unviable or were unfunded. Overall, the significant downturn for all those that supply the energy industry led to major margin pressure. Unfortunately there may yet be more to come, as often the largest projects can only be reviewed once a multi-year expenditure cycle has been completed.

- Indirectly related industries have suffered too. For example, it is much less compelling to buy newer fuel-efficient commercial aircraft when the oil price is low. So there have been many fewer aircraft orders since 2015, with lots of prior orders deferred or cancelled.[34] This has impacted sectors as diverse as aeronautical engineering and software suppliers.

All of these factors have been reflected in a corporate sector that has become constrained with little turnover growth, and disappointing profits and cash flow.

Consumers under pressure

When world trade was globalising, corporate growth was good. With the adoption of debt and the doubling of profit margins, corporate cash flow was excellent. Extra cash flow came through in staff pay, extra payments for government in a growing tax take, and extra returns for investors in the form of improving cash for shareholders. Plenty of extra cash for employees and investors made it easy for the electorate to support globalisation because everyone was doing well.

The Global Financial Crisis interrupted the Goldilocks trend. Although there was a major setback, the aggressive stimuli also generated an equally strong recovery. Whilst corporate cash flow moved back to previous norms, the big surprise has been

---

33   *World Energy Investment Outlook.* 2014 Special Report. International Energy Agency, France.

34   Older aircraft tend to be less fuel-efficient, but when energy prices are lower, the differential in running costs between older and newer commercial aircraft is less significant.

how much world growth has stagnated thereafter. The first thought was that this was something of a temporary phase. But the longer it has persisted, the more it has become a point of concern. In the years since 2008, the absence of any significant growth in corporate cash flow has become linked with the inability to pay significant wage growth.

Economic growth has disappointed along the way, but this has swiftly been addressed via extra QE. This may have boosted demand for short periods but gradually it has been recognised that QE hasn't generated any real economic momentum. Even occasional pickups in demand have been distrusted, so many companies have met any need for extra product by drawing on part-time or temporary staff, often in relatively low-wage roles.

Furthermore, the recent decline in the value of sterling has devalued the value of UK wages relative to others overseas. The bottom line is that real wage growth[35] has been conspicuously disappointing since the financial crisis. On average, the OECD now estimates that the UK workforce has actually endured an average cut in real wages of around 10% since 2007.[36] The Greeks have lost out too, though in their case they have suffered absolute wage reductions – but paid in a currency that has remained buoyed up by the northern European economies.

---

35   Real wages are determined after inflation has been deducted.

36   Unemployment itself is significantly higher in Greece. The OECD's 2016 Employment Outlook highlights a 10.41% decline in real wages in Greece, and a decline of 10.37% in the UK. Source: OECD Employment Outlook 2016. July 2016.

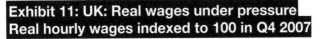

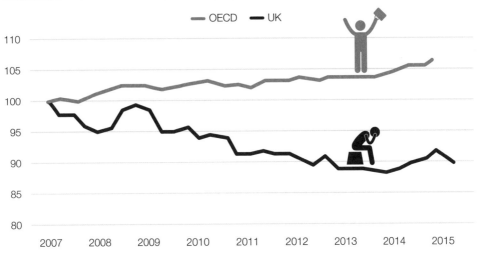

Exhibit 11: UK: Real wages under pressure
Real hourly wages indexed to 100 in Q4 2007

July 2016. Source: OECD Employment Outlook

Given the above it is perhaps unsurprising that attitudes toward globalisation amongst the electorate have hardened over recent years. Many had misgivings in the past – now these have become very real. Even though the UK economy remains in a period of modest growth, the underlying experience has been many finding it harder to make ends meet.

Political pressure on profits

The change in social attitudes will now attract greater political interest. There is more political capital to be made for those proposing caps to household bills and costs. And in general this comes at the expense of corporate margins. For example, prior to the 2015 UK election, the Labour Party proposed a cap on utility bills should it be elected. Most utility suppliers increased their energy-hedging programmes to limit the risk of being caught out with a strong rise in the oil price that they wouldn't be able to pass on to their customers. As it happened, the oil price collapsed thereafter, and some of the extra hedging left the utility companies with commitments to buy energy well *above* the prevailing market price. Some of these costs might have been passed on to customers, since most competitors were in the same position, but ultimately a portion of this extra cost was taken in margin pressure.

In fact there are all sorts of business sectors that may attract political engagement. Many worry over the scale of price increases on some patented medicines in the US and elsewhere. The suppliers of several popular patented pharmaceuticals have been able to increase their prices for many years. This issue attracted political comment when a former hedge fund manager acquired the intellectual rights to manufacture and sell a small specialist drug called Daraprim. It might have been a 62-year-old drug, but it was still crucial for treating a life-threatening parasitic infection. The new owner decided he could game the system by increasing the price of a tablet from $13.50 to $750 overnight, since it was only available from the plant he had acquired.[37] Given the low cost of the acquisition and the blatant profiteering, his actions were seen as outrageous. Politicians required no further evidence to state that they were interested in price-capping a number of the most popular pharmaceutical drugs, especially some of those that had put through the greatest price increases over recent years.

Margin pressure in action

All of these examples point in a consistent direction. There has been a major cultural shift within the attitudes of the electorate. At a time when underlying cash flow is tight, both consumers and companies have become much more price-sensitive in their buying habits. Websites and online auctions make it so much easier to compare a wider range of suppliers' prices. Customers have always expected good value when making purchases. Now they have become more demanding.

Some investors had hoped there would be a greater degree of margin resilience in those industries dominated by a limited number of large competitors. However, when demand flattens, the urgency to attract marginal sales can become overwhelming.

---

37   *Pharmaceuticals: Value over volume.* Financial Times, 24 September 2015.

When the underlying dynamics in a particular sector disappoint, the reduction in sales can quickly come through in extra competitive tension to the point that even the market leaders come under real pressure to cut prices. And once initiated, competitive tit-for-tat discounts quickly drive down corporate margins.

The UK supermarket sector is a prime example. This sector has the advantage of a limited number of competitors, all of whom have taken market share from independents by offering ongoing innovation and a wider range of products. For three decades demand has grown at attractive margins for the operators.

But in spite of mainstream supermarkets taking more market share from the independent sector since 2007, their like-for-like sales turned negative over recent years. In fact, the average UK household spend on food actually fell around 7% between 2007 and 2014.[38] The growth of online deliveries and a move to buy more top-up purchases via local supermarkets magnified the challenge, with the problem being most acute amongst out-of-town stores. When marginal like-for-like sales decline, superstores need millions of pounds of additional sales just to restore sales to the same levels as previous years. So it was inevitable that the combination of historically attractive margins, along with declining sales, would eventually spark a price war – along with all the inevitable consequences.

Once a price war is initiated it is difficult for there to ever be an armistice. When mass-market advertising highlights ever lower prices, it changes the culture of customers. They have become conditioned to expect increasingly competitive prices.

The devaluation of sterling after Brexit could increase prices since even local suppliers can now sell their produce overseas at higher prices. And all suppliers have extra energy and transport costs as well. So all retailers, including supermarkets, are now faced with a rising cost of supplies, at a time when customers have been educated to expect ever more competitive deals. All this adds up to an ongoing period of margin compression, with the pain being shared between the supermarkets and their suppliers.

---

38   Family Food 2014. Department for Environment, Food and Rural Affairs (DEFRA).

We can all smile about the tussle between Unilever and Tesco over the price of a jar of Marmite. But this is the front line of margin compression. In the past mainstream consumer brands have tended to overestimate their ability to sustain a brand premium. And the largest supermarkets have tended to overestimate their customers' loyalty to their specific range and locations. Both have been surprised recently. **Welcome to the world of a profits recession.**

The bottom line is that there are both winners and losers at times like this. If corporate margins do peak out, consumers ultimately get a better deal. But equally, when margins peak out, it is tougher for quoted companies to generate an attractive return for investors. The following chapter outlines the first of a series of fundamental strategy changes that investors will need to make as the retreat of globalisation sets in.

CHAPTER SEVEN:

Aggregate Risks

Investment strategy is now set to change more over the next three years than it has over the last three decades.

Bold policy

A number of earlier chapters touched on the nature of the economic recovery after 2008. This chapter seeks to zero in and assess the degree of investment risk within equity markets, and where that risk might be concentrated. To do so it is useful to start by reflecting on the policies that drove the recovery after 2008, and then follow the logic forward.

The stimulus injected into the economy and markets after 2008 was extreme. Central banks and governments resorted to a policy cocktail of extraordinary intensity:

- The Bank of England had never previously reduced UK interest rates below 2.0% in all the centuries of its existence. Yet the seriousness of the 2008 crisis meant that UK interest rates were reduced from 5.75% to an 'emergency' level of just 0.5%.[39] It is worth lingering on those numbers for a moment. Interest

---

[39] The Bank of England's Official Bank Rate declined from 5.75% on 5 July 2007 to 0.5% on 5 March 2009. Source: Bank of England.

rates approaching 6% sound positively gigantic in a world where commentators speculate as to whether US interest rates might peak at 1.5% or so.

- Central banks anticipated the long-term reduction in bond yields. Therefore the Bank of England, like other central banks, could adopt a policy of greatly narrowing the supply of government bonds, since this merely accelerated the inevitable. It was a stroke of genius, since this policy created extra buyers of corporate bonds and equities and cleared the log-jam of distressed sellers in these exchanges. In the end, the Bank of England purchased about one third of all government borrowings between 2008 and 2015.[40]

Alongside this, the UK government largely sustained state spending at planned levels, even though tax revenues fell sharply with the economic setback of 2008 and 2009. The budget deficit reached 10.8% of GDP in 2009,[41] an unusually large figure for a mainstream economy the size of the UK. However, running a deficit of this magnitude did have a moderating influence on the slowdown to the UK economy at the time.

Overall, these policies were designed to send a jolt of 'shock and awe' to financial markets, so the liquidity gridlock in the exchanges was freed up and an economic depression could be avoided. Fortunately, the Chinese authorities stepped up their investment in Chinese infrastructure too, which also aided world recovery. So although a very large number of corporates ran into a liquidity shortage during the Global Financial Crisis, their problems were often resolved subsequently by greatly reduced borrowing costs, and the fact that they could raise additional debt or equity too, because capital markets were operational.

---

40   UK quantitative easing between 2008 and 2015 amounted to £375bn. Source: Annual Report 2015/2016 Bank of England Asset Purchase Facility Fund.

41   Riley, J. and Chote, R. September 2014. *Crisis and consolidation in the public finances.* Office for Budgetary Responsibility.

Stimulating a recovery

It is interesting to note how quickly the world recovery came through after 2008. It arrived more quickly than expected, with many corporates becoming more cash-generative faster than anticipated. In fact, within a couple of years, most corporates had recovered to their previous norms of profitability.

At this stage, everything appeared set for a conventional economic recovery. With corporate profitability strong, and underlying cash generation going well, it seemed that there might be a solid platform for a renewed burst of capital expenditure. There was a hope that investment in research and development of novel products and services would increase. Alongside this, there was excellent scope for renewed productivity improvement through incremental increases in capital expenditure. The financial picture looked promising.

One way to assess the scale of the opportunity at this time is via the metric of dividend cover.[42] Over time this can be viewed as a measure of corporate potential. At times when dividend cover is rising, or is high, it implies there is plenty of corporate cash flow to fund wage rises, government tax take, and capital expenditure to improve productivity. Conversely, at times when the ratio is falling, or it is at low levels, it implies corporate cash flow is under stress, and indeed there is a risk that dividends could be cut.

The chart in exhibit 12 shows dividend cover for the companies in the FTSE All-Share Index. Note that whilst the ratio did suffer an extreme setback in 2008 and 2009, the speed of the subsequent recovery was remarkable. The central bank and government policies of 'shock and awe' worked incredibly well. Dividend cover, and by implication corporate cash flow, rose back above long-term norms within just a couple of years of the crisis.

---

42   Dividend cover is calculated by taking the annual earnings per share and dividing it by the annual dividend. Higher dividend covers are regarded to be safer than lower dividend covers.

Exhibit 12: UK equities: Dividend cover recovered strongly following the crisis in 2008

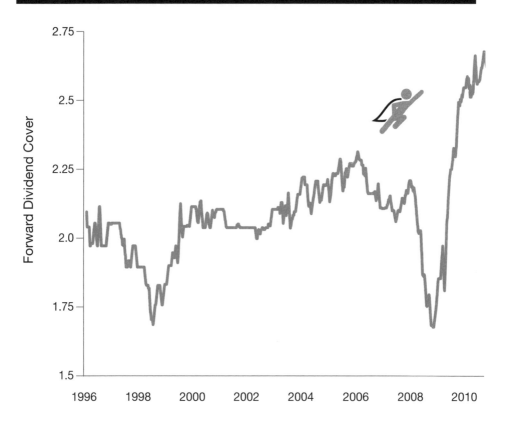

December 2015. Source: Panmure Gordon, Thomson Reuters

Most companies were upbeat about the scope for economic recovery at the time, and many started to increase their dividends to investors. However, almost immediately markets ran into a major setback. Greece was struggling with excess debt and there was a risk that this would force the country to leave the euro. If Greece had exited the euro then many European banks would have been vulnerable to another meltdown, since their balance sheets were still not strong enough to take major write-offs on their holdings of Greek assets. After some negotiations, a Greek bailout package was agreed, and alongside this the authorities stated they were ready to inject extra liquidity into markets as necessary.

Disappointment in the real economy

However, although equity markets have continued to perform well since that time, the economic recovery has been somewhat less buoyant. Economic growth has consistently disappointed, other than in China. In fact, almost irrespective of the scale of the ongoing monetary or fiscal stimulus, world growth has slowed since 2011.

In particular, it is notable that capital expenditure has been disappointing during the economic recovery. Despite plenty of access to low-cost debt, and buoyant exchanges ready to fund growth, most management teams of quoted companies have just not taken the decision to invest heavily in the future. In part, this might be related to the fact that economic prospects haven't been as strong as hoped. In part, it may be related to anxiety over the outlook for their individual markets. In part, it might also reflect the fact that ultra-low interest rates have exacerbated some internal shortfalls, like pensions deficits.

It's important to highlight how significant this will become in time. The current cash flow within businesses relies heavily on their previous history of capital investment. Capital investment helps keep the ranges of products up-to-date and innovative, and keeps sales moving forward, sometimes at premium prices. Investment in incremental productivity improvements drives growth in production and helps to keep unit costs falling.

If anything, the premium yield on quoted companies is what has been driving share prices higher. With economic growth disappointing, most central banks have kept ultra-low interest rates in place for years longer than originally anticipated. And when there have been economic setbacks, many central banks have quickly resorted to additional QE. So whilst corporates might have been under-investing, they have continued to have access to plentiful liquidity. There is a period when a business might actually be generating cash whilst its capital expenditure and interest costs are sub-normal. However this is merely a phase, because after a while the lack of capital expenditure will be reflected in a progressive decline in the profitability and cash flow generated by the company.

The overall effect of these adverse trends has been a deterioration of dividend cover since 2011. In particular, the ongoing lack of productivity improvement has weighed down recent years. Over the last five years, dividend cover has moved from an unusually healthy level to an unusually unhealthy level.

Quite a few quoted companies have been caught out by the slowdown in world growth, and some have inadvertently moved into a position where they are over-distributing dividends. Many are keeping their dividend payments going for now, despite the cash cost of the dividend payment exceeding the underlying cash needed to pay it. For short periods, shortfalls like this can be made up from additional borrowing, but it isn't a sustainable position, especially when investment in improving productivity is sub-normal.

The chart reinforces the point – the current level of dividend payments is close to the lowest margin of safety it has been at for over 20 years. The implications are very serious. During the boom the chart was mainly rising, and this implied that most mainstream quoted companies were relatively good investments. There were setbacks, but the risk of too much corporate decay in 2008 necessitated exceptional monetary and fiscal stimulus and this ultimately came through in a further period of market return. So even during the setbacks, investors were largely protected from the worst downside risks.

But the current level of dividend cover implies that investment risk is very elevated at present. The cash flow generated by many quoted companies is already largely committed to meeting their current commitments. However, the demands on companies are continuing to rise. The lack of wage growth is leading to growing militancy within some groups of employees for the first time in decades. And certainly customers are becoming much more price-sensitive, which could be reflected in wider pressure on corporate profit margins. Alongside this, national governments are becoming more desperate about pressure within their budgets as well. This is prompting governments to impose national tax claims on multinationals. Exhibit 13 implies that there is serious pressure of further dividend cuts in future.

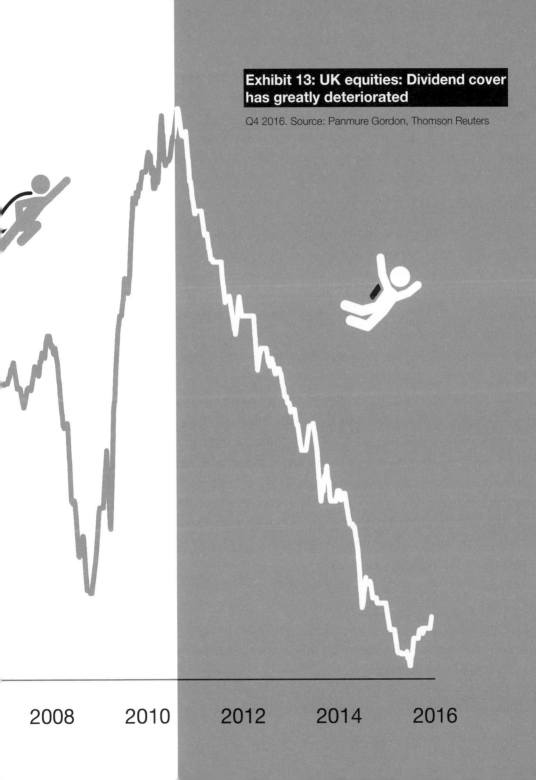

Exhibit 13: UK equities: Dividend cover has greatly deteriorated

Q4 2016. Source: Panmure Gordon, Thomson Reuters

2008   2010   2012   2014   2016

In fact, even marginal corporate disappointments are often being reflected in dividend cuts. There are specific corporate reasons for each, linked in part to the collapse of the commodity cycle, the price wars in the supermarkets and specific margin pressure in some other industries. But note that these dividend cuts are coming through *in spite* of the fact that UK interest rates have remained at remarkably low levels.

Running out of stimuli

After 2008 the central banks might have even surprised themselves with the efficacy of their policies. When it comes to closing a door very quietly, the degree of control tends to be so much better if the handle is pulled whilst the door is pushed gently at the same time. The implementation of extraordinarily aggressive economic factors, together with the rapid growth of the Chinese economy after 2008, have given the central bankers an apparently fine degree of control to manage the financial recovery. At times when exchanges picked up, they scaled back monetary stimulus. And when economic data led to a market wobble, the authorities reached for more QE as necessary.

But more recently the lack of a robust and sustained economic recovery is making central banks around the world increasingly desperate. Some have been exploring negative interest rate regimes in spite of the fact that they come with severe economic drawbacks. In particular, negative interest rates undermine the viability of banks, and they make the management of future liabilities for pension funds near impossible. A negative return on bonds implies that pension schemes need more assets now than the total sums they are due to pay out in pension payments in the future. Worse still, if there were to be another significant economic setback, the opportunity for monetary policy actions by central banks is now largely exhausted. Most central banks have used up their firepower addressing the problems of the previous Global Financial Crisis.

Far from central banks being all-powerful, the reality is that they are not well-placed to engineer another solid market recovery should there be another major setback. In particular this is because:

- QE works best through reducing long duration interest rates and encouraging additional investment by corporates. After many years of QE, and after Brexit, the yields on long-dated UK gilts are close to multi-decade lows. The position overseas is if anything even more unsettling, with some government bond yields standing below zero.

- Meanwhile, the UK government is still trying to get the country's annual budget back in balance after it became greatly overstretched at the time of the Global Financial Crisis. The process of paring back government expenditure to bring it into balance with government revenues is proving much harder than anticipated – and has been met with limited support from the electorate. There is little room for the UK government to deliberately step up overspend again in future.

- The wide-ranging global recovery was greatly assisted by China's decision to radically step up its infrastructure spend. But with the boom in Chinese infrastructure already beyond its peak, it seems fair to expect a slower rate of growth going forward.

Overall, lack of productivity improvement is at the centre of our collective problem. If anything, corporate cash flow could become even more constrained in future, which could hold up capital expenditure even for those companies that have attractive opportunities.

All this implies that the investment strategies that have worked well over the last three decades could carry a lot more risk in future. The first part of this book has outlined how social attitudes can and do change markedly at times. Changes in the social and political landscape tend to lead to major change in economic policy. And ultimately these are later reflected in a major change in market trends. We are now at that point where the status quo has become too risky. Investors need to be a lot more attentive to downside risk going forward. Investment strategy is set to change more over the next three years than it has over the last three decades. The following chapters address the implications head on.

CHAPTER EIGHT:

Turn and Face the Change

It may be that the financial markets became overly sophisticated during the credit booms. Simple straightforward investment strategies based on individuals actively selecting the best have the advantage of being more effective and understandable.

Outsized corporate profits along with a degree of corporate imprudence, central bank salvation along with central bank distortions, two credit booms, along with pressures on profits and corporate cash flow going forward – this is where we find ourselves after three decades since the last great change in economic trends. These are certainly not the only ways in which the world has been changed. But they are important because their implications are so significant going forward.

The first seven chapters of this book have looked at how the business world has been transformed over the past 30 years. It has also drawn attention to how that transformation could change going forward. More recently, changes in social and political attitudes are injecting a degree of change in economic and market trends. This marks a major shift in the trajectory of the global economy compared with the past. It also marks an important moment for investors.

Anxiety and the art of asset allocation

Generally the role of institutional fund managers is to ensure that their clients' assets are invested in a portfolio that can generate an attractive return, without incurring too much risk along the way. Naturally managers are attentive to the financial and economic risks that they perceive up ahead, as they intend to steer their clients' capital around the worst of any problems. But fund managers are also cautious of adjusting asset allocation too much, or too fast, because the current market trends have been relatively consistent for decades. One of the most common mistakes within asset allocation is to get over-enthused about an immature trend in its early stages. It is natural for investors to want to participate in new areas of opportunity when they appear. Far too often, however, the development of these new areas doesn't come through as quickly as expected. And when it does, far too often the returns on the novel area turn out to be unremarkable.

A fine example was the dotcom boom around 2000. Most fund managers naturally recognised that the internet would be a major source of commercial advantage in time, and that early adopters could generate some very high potential returns. The question was what portion of client capital should be allocated away from 'old economy' stocks to support novel companies that were hoping to be first movers in the growth of the internet. As most will remember, the share prices of these kinds of companies shot up prior to December 1999, and these returns drew in additional capital from all parts of the investment universe. However, an almost unlimited number of 'me too' fund raisings in the early part of the year 2000 quickly overwhelmed the new capital available. After March 2000, the value of many dotcom stocks dropped nearly as fast as they had risen. In the end, most dotcom companies generated poor returns for investors.

Experiences like these reinforce natural institutional inertia against rushing any major changes to asset allocation. The inclination to stick with the status quo has actually worked out really well for institutional clients over recent decades. Although the deregulation of the debt markets was inflationary, and therefore negative for the valuation of long bonds, this effect was more than offset by the globalisation of world trade.

Valuations have been boosted by falling bond yields

Overall, globalisation has been strongly deflationary – think of the way in which goods produced and assembled in low-cost regimes all over the world have become a tide of cheap imported goods. In investment terms, the globalisation of low-cost goods and services has come to predominate all others. And being deflationary, it has justified the ongoing reduction in bond yields, a trend that has been in place since around 1990.

Exhibit 14: The remarkable decline in UK long bond yields

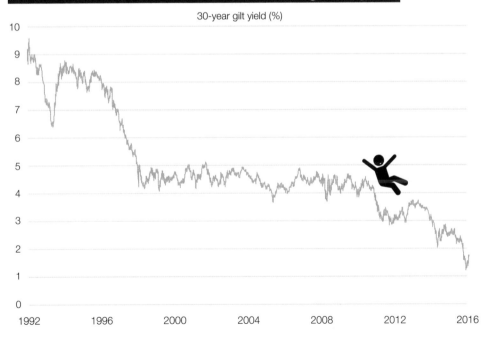

30-year gilt yield (%)

Source: Bloomberg

The valuation of most assets is derived with reference to the yield of long-term bonds. So as long-term bond yields have fallen, the valuation of most assets has greatly increased. During the boom period, returns were exceptional because they were driven by a combination of supernormal corporate sales growth and a rise in the corporate profit margin on those sales, along with an ongoing improvement in valuations.

From an asset allocator's viewpoint, when valuations are rising, there are numerous strategies that can generate an attractive return. Acquisition-led strategies generate good capital gains because one-off synergy benefits are worth a lot when valuation multiples are rising. Good returns can be made on asset-based strategies too, where capital is invested in the rising value of property or another financial asset, especially when paired with significant borrowings. Many investors have simply short-circuited the whole selection process and allocated a large portion of quoted equity holdings in funds based upon benchmark indices.

Clearly asset prices fell back during the Global Financial Crisis. But the emergency fiscal and monetary policies thereafter have driven a remarkable appreciation of equity markets since then. As world growth has stagnated, monetary and fiscal stimuli have become the most significant driver of market returns. If anything, the ongoing reduction in long bond yields has continued to favour investment strategies that were popular during the boom period. There is an important point here: subsequent to the Global Financial Crisis, the rise in asset prices has been the principal driver of returns.

Index funds have fully participated in a rise in markets driven by the ongoing stimulus from monetary and fiscal policy. In particular, their insensitivity to corporate risk has often worked in their favour. Over Brexit, for example, the best returns were generated by index funds once more. Many of the largest multinationals pay their dividends out in US dollars or euros, and these were worth 10% or 15% more in sterling terms after the Brexit devaluation. In general, it is only index funds that would invest between 5% or 10% of a portfolio in individual companies that are greatly over-distributing dividends.

A change in the air

In the past, the success of mainstream incumbents has been positively helpful for index funds. And it has been right for asset allocators to stick with the status quo for almost a generation. But intuitively many already have a sense that index-benchmarked strategies have passed their best. Strategies that allocate with reference to market capitalisation, stock liquidity or acquisition-led growth are clearly less relevant when valuation improvement runs out of steam.

And if stock-specific risk is much more elevated in future, then insensitivity to risk will become the Achilles heel for index-based funds. Going forward, it will be more important than ever to invest with greater attention to downside corporate risk. In future, ultra-low bond yields imply that most asset classes will deliver meagre returns. However, index funds are at risk of delivering sub-normal returns along with heightened volatility.

It is a truism that a strategy that relies on ever falling bond yields and ever rising market valuations cannot be sustainable. A strategy that depends on its insensitivity to corporate risk is unsustainable. The point is that now that bond yields worldwide have reached ultra-low levels, there is little room for any further valuation improvement. Chapter seven concluded with an expectation that all investors are facing an extraordinary period of change ahead.

Alongside this, the problems of slowing productivity (and the fact that corporate cash flow is under pressure) are now coming through in a profound change in social attitudes. This is a new trend that has wrong-footed many political commentators. Recent political upheavals, such as Donald Trump's victory in the 2016 US presidential election, would have been difficult to predict until recently.

The combination of these changes, and the deep-seated nature of the transition, marks an important moment for asset allocators. For the last three decades, it has paid to project trends from the past into the future. But now the greatest risks lie in sticking with the status quo. It's time to consider a profound and wide-ranging shift in the long-term economic trajectory. Therefore prepare for asset allocation to go through its biggest period of change in decades.

Anticipating change

My two previous books advocated investment strategies for sustaining attractive returns whilst there was a broad slowdown in world growth. These strategies remain valid. However, time has moved on and we have reached a point where social and political attitudes are changing as well. This book seeks to underline the deep-seated nature of this progression and give a glimpse of how the changing views will be reflected in the evolution of economic and market trends.

The problem with the end of the status quo is not identifying which strategies carry too much risk and now need to be sold. Rather, at a time when corporate risk is greatly elevated it is more important than ever to have a clear view of the metrics that can help identify the right strategies for the future.

It is hard to overstate the scale of this change. For example, over the last three decades the effectiveness of most funds has been determined by reference to total returns. Many investors in equity income funds have been very attentive as to overall total returns, comprising both the income received and the associated capital appreciation of their funds. For many years, a majority of the returns has been driven by the growth and appreciation of quoted stocks rather than dividend income.

But going forward, when market returns could be so much more temporal, trading strategies chasing capital gains will be much more risky. Generally strategies that rely on general market appreciation won't generate much return, and may suffer considerable volatility along the way. In future, a much more relevant yardstick will be the ongoing underlying income growth these funds deliver. The ongoing growth of cash flow within the portfolio holdings, driven by productivity improvement, will be a much more important metric of long-term return. In addition, strategies based on maximising underlying dividend growth are also likely to be much more stable and consistent – something that will become valued in itself when markets themselves may be much more volatile.

Strategies like this can be described as '**allocation for outcome**'. Expect asset allocators to move away from index funds and exchange-traded funds (ETFs), towards funds where it is the operational characteristics of the individual stocks that become the main focus. Portfolios like this will be defined by metrics that have been generally underplayed during the boom years. Equally, these kinds of strategies will tend to be much more sensitive and deliberate in the risks they tolerate within portfolios. Ultimately sustained and growing cash flow derived from ongoing capital expenditure could become the key yardstick in future. The long-term progress of these strategies can then be reported against these metrics.

Improving corporate efficiency

When investment returns have been so good for so long, marginal corporate inefficiencies are easy to overlook. Alongside this, the long-term rise in corporate margins has helped to obscure incidences where central costs may have become too inflated. When most companies are successful, some can tolerate excessive internal complexity because overall returns are still satisfactory. In the past the more important driver of return has been related to how much leverage has been involved, or how quickly an acquisition has generated a return. Organic productivity improvement has been just one of several strategies that generated a return.

But going forward, as investment returns are more limited, the level of internal efficiency will become a lot more relevant. Equally, as organic productivity improvement becomes a more popular strategy with investors, the justification for every part of the corporate overhead will become more closely challenged.

In particular, as investment strategies move towards outcome-orientated investment strategies, companies that have become weakened due to too little spending on innovative research and development will fall from favour. Those that let corporate productivity slow so there is too little operational efficiency improvement will come under pressure.

These issues are not just about a renewed focus on commercial purpose, or a greater interest in organic growth. Rather it will just be a move back to steadier, less risky corporate strategies. At times of great opportunity, it seemed relatively dull to eke out marginal gains by reducing the complexity of overhead structures. When profit margins were high, companies spent time assessing the prospects for building the scale of the business, rather than worrying about getting the organisation humming on a steady-state basis. One of the main problems that Dave Lewis outlined when he was appointed the new chief executive of Tesco was that head office relied on data from customer-facing staff. So as the business ran into trouble, head office asked customer-facing staff to spend more and more time collecting data for head office, rather than getting on with their main role of looking after their customers.

There is bags of room for improvements in operational efficiency within corporates now that world growth has slowed.

Index funds

For years those firms that were insufficiently cash-generative to meet all of their financial commitments were able to access easy liquidity in the markets. In general, corporates might have become overly dependent on the ultra-low cost of debt over the boom. To date debt has enhanced the returns for shareholders since valuations have been rising, as long-term bond yields have declined. Some believe that easy liquidity conditions will remain supportive into the future, so debt can be a core part of long-term corporate funding plans. This assumption implies corporates have no reason to generate cash from their operations to repay their loans. And as interest rates have been trending toward zero, it's easy to equate the cost of debt as 'free'. To date historic obligations to repay debt have been met by raising new debt to repay the previous lenders.

But now that world growth has stagnated, and economic and market trends are changing, there are risks that large debt balances could become very problematic. Debt tends to exaggerate underlying trends, so an adverse trading period within a geared capital structure will lead to a severe bottleneck in demands for cash. The time when lenders become unsettled often coincides with the time when other corporates scale back the credit they provide. In addition, those with significant debt due for repayment during an economic downturn can find it much harder to borrow the same sum again. So economic downturns are normally marked by a pick up in corporate failures. It seems very likely that downside risk will be much more severe in future.

In summary, corporate risk was a contributor to returns during the credit boom, but this leaves far too many poorly positioned to address a major change in economic trends. Both of the previous sections have highlighted how a change in investment mindset can help investors continue to generate attractive returns and better manage their risks going forward. But this also implies that the right investment strategy for the future should avoid averages. Index funds might have been successful when markets were generating consistent returns. But both index funds and ETFs are marked by their insensitivity to stock-specific risk. This just isn't the time to buy funds that lack conviction in their 8% holdings.

In future, investors need to select holdings for their resilience and productivity improvements, rather than their plentiful liquidity or large index weightings. After all, ultra-low bond yields imply that forthcoming market returns will be sub-normal. And market volatility may be more challenging as well. Investors can be expected to greatly reduce their use of all passive fund structures going forward. Index funds work best during booms, but at other times they are too risk-insensitive. Long-term investment in index funds has passed its sell-by date.

Spin-off benefits of the new allocation trends

In future, asset allocation will move towards strategies that are more deliberate in the way they achieve returns. This period of fundamental political, economic, and market change will mark a time when the fund management sector has the opportunity to have a hand in minimising the adverse consequences of corporate failure. As globalisation moves into retreat, the adoption of these kinds of strategies will demonstrate the social utility of the financial sector. Encouraging companies to prioritise productivity improvement and hold more robust balance sheets is a way of preparing for a risk of more corporate casualties. The best prepared will be ready and waiting to grow in the voids that might open up.

Expect many investment strategies to evolve towards a wider opportunity set through this process. It might be positively advantageous to stretch the investment universe beyond the limits of index constituents. When fewer individual companies are set to generate an attractive return, it's logical to adopt a strategy that widens the opportunity set. Portfolios can steer round those with too much corporate risk more easily, as well as increasing the potential to back those with better return potential. Following QE and ultra-low interest rates, almost all asset markets have become extraordinarily correlated. So, in future, it will be more important than ever to adopt an investment strategy that is less in sync with market indices.

The way forward is not just about making plans to better withstand any financial challenges ahead. It's also about actively funding those that will derive additional opportunity as the forest canopy opens up. These transitions will be even more important in the UK as any adverse global trend will be overlaid with extra economic disruption as the UK leaves the EU. Some overseas investors may hold back a proportion, possibly even a sizeable proportion, of their ongoing UK investment until the terms of the new trade arrangements are known. Equally, some multinationals may move their head offices to elsewhere in the EU. Both of these factors could lead to challenges. The consistent support of a better balance in our corporate forest will make a real difference to the success of the UK economy. Essentially, fund managers will be favouring and facilitating sustained supply-side reform.

This is a big opportunity. The allocation of our collective savings is going through a period of radical change. Expect many more funds to advocate prioritising corporate productivity improvement in future. This isn't just about strategies that will carry less risk, it's about strategies that are more independent of rising valuations driven by ever lower bond yields. Importantly, it will ensure our businesses are more resilient and better positioned to generate sustained cash paybacks too. Well-invested companies are well-placed to fund additional employment and tax take, as well as ongoing dividend growth.

This is a very important moment for all investors, but most particularly our financial institutions. Our fund management industry is at the centre of the allocation of our collective savings. Overall it may get harder to generate an attractive return for our savers. However, the most able, active fund managers will adopt strategies similar to those advocated here so that they can actively support those with the best productivity improvement in prospect.

All this marks a profound change in trend, whereby our collective risk capital is being steered away from the allocation trends of the past three decades towards improving our overall corporate cash flow going forward. But what kinds of companies might sustain attractive profit margins at a time when most are cutting their prices? How can good companies steer round a profits recession? The following chapters address these questions in a little more detail.

CHAPTER NINE:

Niche is Nice

There are always some stocks that can resist margin pressure by operating in niche areas where demand is growing on a secular basis.

Narrowing down on niches

There are several reasons why longer-term trends point to an upcoming period of corporate margin compression. Finding companies that are best placed to withstand this kind of hostile environment may not be an especially familiar task. During the credit boom, the rising tide lifted many boats and the years of exceptional stimulus after 2008 insulated financial markets from the worst of margin compression in the commodity sectors: indices simply continued to rise elsewhere.

Many investors seeking to avoid margin pressure might initially assume that technology stocks with novel products would be a promising area in which to begin. But the problem with technological success is that it is often transient. Technological leaders can be usurped within a few years. Nokia and BlackBerry were the dominant mobile phone companies on the world stage for quite some time, but this position was lost shortly thereafter. Even the gigantic and relatively long-lived success of

Apple, through its innovation in computing and assorted mobile technologies, is currently coming under question[43] – though both Apple and Microsoft are close to being unique as they have sustained their technological edges and very sizeable cash flows for many years.

Alongside this, ultimately nearly all technology stocks fail to live up to these inflated expectations and the share price returns on most growth stocks disappoint.[44] So seeking to identify businesses that can resist margin pressure via innovative technologies is unlikely to be an especially resilient strategy at a time of margin pressure.

However, there are other areas that could be more fruitful. **It is all about identifying companies that customers have an active reason for continuing to support.** There are always some stocks that can resist margin pressure by operating in niche areas where demand is growing on a secular basis.

For example, whilst mainstream supermarkets in the UK may be under pressure, there are still some niche grocery markets that remain relatively buoyant. For instance, there is a growing number of people happy to pay premium prices for premium products. Marks & Spencer's UK supermarkets reflect this trend through positive like-for-like sales at a time when mainstream supermarkets are discounting their prices to retain sales. Waitrose[45] is also expanding in this premium niche too.

Likewise, there is a 'no-frills' niche for those who are happy to buy from a narrower range of product lines but where the prices of the items stocked are below the mainstream supermarkets. This is an area where non-listed names like Aldi and Lidl[46] have been profitably expanding – despite the general margin pressure in the mainstream supermarket sector.

---

43   *Apple reports first quarterly sales drop since 2003 as iPhone stumbles.* Wall Street Journal, 26 April 2016.

44   Growth stocks have high valuation ratios, with shares reflecting anticipated future cash flows. Studies in the UK and US suggest that cumulative returns over longer timescales from stocks with these characteristics tend to be lower than from value stocks, which are perceived to have less exciting prospects. See Elroy Dimson, Paul Marsh, Mike Staunton. *Credit Suisse Global Investment Returns Sourcebook.* 2012. London Business School.

45   Waitrose is part of the John Lewis Partnership and therefore not part of a publicly quoted company.

46   Aldi and Lidl are both private companies and therefore unavailable for those investing in quoted stocks.

So certain corporates can generate good and sustained corporate profit margins in niche markets, with growth in sales and cash flow. Clearly these kinds of niches will attract greater inward investment from 'me-too' competitors. But often dominant players in a specific niche can keep ahead of new entrants, given their established positions and through taking advantage of scale efficiencies to generate good and sustained margins over the longer term – all leading to an attractive rate of return for shareholders.

Small and immature – and ideal

Niches can be quite substantive in terms of sales and profits (as they are in the UK grocery market), but niches are – by definition – typically specialist fields that are minority areas compared to the mainstream. This makes it harder for the very largest companies to identify niche markets that are sizeable enough to drive the return on their overall business. So whereas the Marks & Spencer food shops have been a conspicuous success over recent years, the average Marks & Spencer plc shareholder has not enjoyed particularly good returns on his or her investment. The trajectory of the M&S share price is principally related to results in its clothing business since its supermarket niche only accounts for a minority of its sales.

All this points towards the fact that those looking to invest in niche companies with the prospect of good and sustained margins will normally need to consider investing in smaller businesses that are coming through from less-established parts of the market. It is helpful that there are many smaller quoted companies that are, on the whole, single product companies. If a firm's product or service is relevant to customers and happens to be in a lucrative niche, it is likely that its share prices will outperform – if the business generates attractive margins on a growing sales line for a decent number of years.

The second advantage of an increased willingness to invest in companies outside the mainstream is the tendency of these businesses to be relatively immature relative to the wider market. Both Aldi and Lidl have been operating in their niche of the UK grocery market for well over a decade, and yet they still have a relatively modest portion of it. It is often the immaturity of smallness that can offer long-term advantages since those that get it right can go on to deliver premium returns for an extended period.

Identifying niche companies with good prospects is a positive strategy to pursue, especially at a time when corporate profit margins are coming under pressure. But niches by definition are a minority of many markets. Not all niche companies will be well run, others will be expensive and some won't be that promising, so it can be difficult to fully populate a diversified portfolio with niche companies. In itself, this strategy is but one of a number that appear well-placed to address the worst of a period of margin compression. The following chapters will cover two more mainstream strategies that can be applied to both large and small quoted companies.

Examples of growing niches

- Leisure – certain parts of internet gaming, experience-based consumption, 'pay-as-you-go' fitness services.

- Food retail – convenience foods, 'clean' or unadulterated foods, 'functional' foods with alleged health benefits.

- Health – treatments for 'lifestyle' diseases, including diabetes and obesity, dietary supplements, male skincare, self-monitoring devices.

- Financials – mobile payment services, lending services targeted at over 65s, targeted insurance services.

- Technology – some parts of cloud services, cyber security markets and wearable technology.

- Workplace regulation – health and safety requirements.

- Industry – recycling as production processes become cyclical not linear.

CHAPTER TEN:

Productivity Improvement

One of the surest methods of securing an attractive return is through investing in quoted companies with a dividend yield that grows well over forthcoming years. Prioritising companies making productivity improvements does this in spades.

The ultimate driver of return

During the boom, the outstanding returns derived from mainstream stocks led to a whole generation of fund managers associating largeness and maturity with growth and easy market liquidity. Indeed, most have come to believe that investments in quoted companies outside of those in mainstream indices are merely of minority interest. Most have no worry over a near-zero long-term allocation to this universe. Regular equity portfolios are considered perfectly viable when investing solely within the FTSE 350.

Over the boom, institutional investment in companies that find themselves outside of the mainstream indices gradually faded. This attitude became so entrenched that most professional investors wouldn't even consider meeting the management teams of companies that didn't form part of the FTSE 350 – irrespective of their investment fundamentals. The institutions knew they wouldn't invest, however good their opportunity.

And yet this attitude is at odds with one of the main drivers of investment return over the very long term. Returns on assets are typically determined by just two factors – the initial yield on the asset at purchase, and how much the regular cash payments change thereafter. If there's ongoing dividend growth, this drives a sustained capital gain. The long-term return often amounts to the rate of dividend growth plus the initial yield. Conversely, if dividends are cut, this often comes through in declines in asset prices.

Clearly the valuation of a quoted business changes every day, so many investors seek to time their purchases and sales of shares, buying when prices are low, and hopefully selling them at a higher level sometime later. However, whilst the valuation of the market does change from year to year, over the longer term, it tends to fluctuate within a band. So over the longer term, the fluctuations of valuation become less and less relevant to the overall return.

One of the most surefooted ways to make an attractive return on stocks is therefore to purchase equity in a business that invests capital on internal projects that generate productivity improvement. Ultimately it is the growing stream of cash returns from these productivity improvements that really drives wealth generation. The ongoing payback in the form of a growing cash flow drives sustainable share price appreciation over time. Cash flow is the key, with annual dividends often the outward manifestation of the underlying growth in the cash generated within a business.

During the credit boom there was plenty of capital investment going on within companies. When markets are growing rapidly, there are lots of good reasons to invest. It was to be expected that this trend would be interrupted with the Global Financial Crisis, when corporate cash flow fell back abruptly. However, with the strong improvement in corporate profitability and underlying cash flow after 2008, it was assumed that there was room for a recovery in corporate investment and productivity improvement. There was a hope that investment in research and development of novel products and services would recover again.

This is easier to achieve for those with plenty of internal cash being generated. But even for those with limited internal cash flow, there was plenty of inexpensive corporate liquidity available. It was expected that capital investment in productivity would progressively recover.

Something else happened.

Corporate productivity as a flywheel

Capital investment in a business can be likened to a flywheel, which plays a balancing role in an engine. Whilst capital investment can pause for the odd few years here and there, ultimately all corporates need to keep funding significant investment in the future, so the flywheel doesn't slow too much. Without ongoing capital investment, a company's commercial advantage will gradually be undermined.

And yet, far too many corporates have not been investing sufficiently since 2008. Despite plentiful access to debt at ultra-low interest rate levels, plus buoyant share prices to fund the needs of quoted companies, few corporates have invested significant sums in productivity improvement. Organic improvement to productivity has been consistently disappointing since 2008.

Strangely enough, in stock market terms, the subdued level of capital investment hasn't been an immediate problem. Those companies that held back on capital expenditure have tended to build up a surplus of cash in their businesses. But this is at odds with the fact that the productivity flywheel, which is the long-term source of corporate cash flow, may be continuing to slow. For short periods, cash flow shortfalls can be made up from additional borrowing. But this isn't a sustainable position, especially when underlying investment in productivity improvement is sub-normal.

Now the accumulated lack of investment in productivity improvement is starting to weigh, and the benefits of exceptional stimulus are fading into the past, so corporate cash flow has tightened. The longer that capital investment is held back, the greater our collective long-term problem. The current cash flow within businesses is often derived from the aggregate investment of the past. But as the previous capital investment ages, the remaining return gradually fades. Corporate cash flow will gradually drop away in the absence of ongoing incremental capital investment.

There is a direct link between disappointing cash flow from corporates, downward pressure on wages and the collective views of the electorate. Social attitudes have changed, and electoral preferences are now coming through in a new political consensus.

Selecting for productivity improvement

One of the advantages of being quoted is that companies can improve their returns for investors through raising additional capital to invest in projects that incrementally improve their businesses. During the credit boom there were many opportunities for generating an attractive return on capital, and capital expenditure was but one. However, if market returns are constrained in future, most of the alternative methods are unlikely to be as attractive. Investing in a rising asset, especially using a geared capital structure incorporating a significant amount of debt, clearly only works well when asset prices are rising. Equally, buying back shares funded by extra debt only really delivers value to shareholders if trading conditions are benign.

So at a time when underlying economic growth is limited, and there is a risk that corporate margins will be under pressure, there is all the greater reason for investors to prioritise investing in companies that have good scope for productivity improvements. After all, companies generating productivity improvements are well-placed to enjoy some benefit from reduced unit costs. They might have slightly greater scope to take some market share as well.

These types of projects tend to comprise a period of investment, followed by a period of enhanced profitability as the extra cash flow more than repays the original investment. Some projects are colossal, requiring several billion pounds, with the prospect of very substantial profitability in future. For example, the development of an offshore oil field in the North Sea typically involves many years of seismic surveys and the drilling of exploration wells before the prospective developer can be confident there is a major oil field in place. Thereafter, it still involves a very substantial development plan, with further production wells explored as well.

It is not unusual for this process to take ten years or more, and only after that period does the project move into profit and start to generate cash. Long-term projects like this often need to generate a total return that is several multiples of the original investment. The overall cost is not just a sum of all the capital invested but should include the returns forgone on that capital had it been invested elsewhere over that period. Major projects like this can generate terrific returns, but only over the very long term.

In contrast, some companies can invest a relatively small sum in slightly speeding an internal process with the improvement in profitability coming through almost immediately. The improvement in profitability and cash flow from these types of projects might be relatively small. But they have the huge advantage that the additional uplift in profitability comes through relatively quickly.

An offshore oil field development would typically generate a much larger return on the original capital, often expressed as the internal rate of return (IRR). Clearly, a higher IRR can appear to be a better investment prospect than a project with a lower IRR. However, this calculation doesn't express the true nature of the risk being undertaken on a project. An oil company that initiated a major oil field development ten years ago might only be getting the project up and running now. In the intervening period, the world has suffered a Global Financial Crisis, and more recently the oil price has collapsed. These kinds of factors would naturally have a major bearing on just how much profit and cash flow is generated by the new oil field. And in this case, the assumptions made at the start of the project could well appear overoptimistic in retrospect.

So whilst many smaller iterative projects might have lower IRRs, they often tend to generate profitability and cash flow payback very quickly. This leaves less scope for the original assumptions about the project to turn out to be overoptimistic. Overall, modest capex projects tend to have much lower risks and contribute to much quicker improvements in the underlying profitability of a business.

Cash payback periods

When assessing companies regarding their capital investment for productivity improvement, it is therefore often worth concentrating on the cash payback period in preference to the internal rate of return. The cash payback period is the period between the first commitment of capital and the time when the underlying cash flow from the project has grown to exceed the original sum invested. Cash paybacks are crucial.

Typically, smaller projects generate a cash payback of around three years. Sometimes projects that generate a cash payback of four or five years are approved, often because they are considered to have unusually low risks, or are urgently required to keep the business competitive with others. At a time when social and political attitudes are changing, it seems appropriate to prioritise those companies with capital projects on short payback periods over those with higher internal rates of return that stretch off further into the future.

Ultimately the great advantage of those that invest capital successfully is that the stream of extra profit and cash flow derived doesn't normally cease at the end of the payback period. It is usually the case that the enhancement continues to generate ongoing profit and cash flow for an extended period. This is very helpful for funding better wages for the staff, and more tax take for the government, at a time when others may be struggling. And it also puts the company in a good position to step up its dividends to long-term investors once the cash payback period has been passed.

All this links back to the driver of return outlined at the start of the chapter. One of the surest methods of securing an attractive return is through investing in quoted companies with an annual dividend that grows well over the forthcoming years. Prioritising companies making productivity improvements does this in spades.

CHAPTER ELEVEN:

Superior Service Standards for Superior Returns

The best companies can only generate premium margins on premium service levels if they continuously eliminate costs without compromising on standards.

High standards – high prices

There are good reasons to invest in companies with outstanding service standards at any time. Those with commercial products and superior service standards often grow and prosper because they generate better profit margins and more cash flow than others.

However, top-drawer service standards are not an end in themselves. There are plenty of companies that can put together teams of staff who notionally offer top-of-the-range service levels. Think of all those high-end country hotels that have never made a commercial profit. The problem for investors is that some companies offering high service levels never win sufficient customers to generate sales in the volumes they need to make their businesses viable.

The really attractive businesses are those where the excellent service levels are truly valuable to customers, and where customers in ever increasing numbers are happy to pay premium prices as well.

At times of general margin pressure, most businesses are condemned to suffer an adverse margin trend. It is important for investors to pay special attention to those that can justify the prices they charge for delivering outstanding service standards – they have a real chance of bucking that trend. But how can an informed investor correctly identify those that have the promising mix of both volume growth and premium margins?

In my career I have met a large number of company management teams; in general, those that are best aligned with the needs of their customers tend to be those that best justify premium pricing. This may sound a little trite. After all, most companies like to think they are good businesses with happy customers who are broadly comfortable with their pricing. However, in my experience this is often not the case. All businesses have a hierarchy of priorities. Fine-tuning the corporate offer to closely reflect the needs of customers is just one of a multitude of needs – along with loan refinancing, questions over internal audits, retaining and recruiting staff, reporting to shareholders and so on.

When meeting companies it is worth finding out exactly how they choose to measure their customer service. It often reveals exactly where the everyday needs of customers are ranked in relation to all the other business necessities. **In my view, it is only those companies that are wholly in tune with their customers that can really justify service levels priced at a premium.** If that is the case, attractive margins and profitable growth are more likely.

How to measure service

There is a very wide range of quoted companies and an equally wide range of ways to measure customer service – the key is to assess the level of priority the management team places on customer service. Many companies use the percentage of products delivered in full and on time as a measure of customer service, for example. This is a useful measure to compare service levels across a sector, and to some degree across industry sectors too.

Another relatively standard way to measure customer service is via the incidence of complaints. However, many customers who are slightly dissatisfied with service levels don't complain formally. It often takes a particularly bad experience to motivate a customer to make a formal complaint; as such customer complaints can represent just the tip of an iceberg of customer dissatisfaction.

A potential follow-up question might aim to assess how well customer service information is compiled to ensure that good management decisions are made. For example, I often ask how much of a company's monthly board pack is made up of details regarding service levels. Whilst the absolute level of customer service is informative, the really interesting data relates to how much that level fluctuates over time. Some service levels can justifiably fluctuate on a month-by-month basis. To take a simple example, a logistics business is likely to find that its service levels are compromised when the national road network is affected by an extended period of freezing weather.

In general, though, good businesses keep service levels at a high level for the majority of the time, with the aim to improve them further when they can. Rising levels of complaints are almost always a worrying development for investors. It usually means that there has been a dip in service levels which customers believe is down to the inefficiency of the supplier. Some customers also back up their complaints with a refusal to pay final invoices.

Exhibit 15: An iceberg of dissatisfaction

Often a rise in complaints leads to customers moving to other suppliers, thereby depressing the underlying growth dynamic of a business. It frequently leads to margin pressure too, as the company is forced to scale down its final invoices to make up for deficiencies elsewhere. Always take note if service levels dip significantly for any reason: this will be reflected in a dip in corporate revenues and margins, particularly if the trend remains in place for a sustained period.

It is worth noting that premium service changes over time. For it to remain at a premium, it needs to evolve in ways that are relevant to the customer experience. Equally, the most attuned companies will be able to scale back those operations that have become less relevant or irrelevant to the customer, minimising costs to keep pricing appropriate too.

The very best companies are those that are very good at identifying the right ways to deliver full value to their customers and yet match this with a highly efficient cost base. But even these can only generate premium margins on premium service if they are also constantly finding processes and costs that can be eliminated without compromising the service standards of their customers.

Finally, there are extra advantages for companies that use their customer-specific data and then lay it out as evidence of their high service levels when they are discussing a potential renewal of an existing contract. Having this kind of data to hand tends to give the business the best chance of justifying current pricing levels and thereby offsetting any margin pressure that might be applied by the customer.

As noted at the beginning of the chapter, there are good reasons to invest in companies with exceptional service standards at any time. But with the risk of a profits recession, first-rate service may be even more important than usual. Companies that sustain their margins can generate additional cash flow even with small rises in turnover. Remember, one of the surest methods of securing an attractive return is through investing in quoted companies with scope to grow their dividends over the forthcoming years. At a time when many other quoted companies may struggle just to sustain cash flow, those with outstanding service levels and rising cash flow could really stand out.

CHAPTER TWELVE:

Risk Reduction

It is important to widen the opportunity set to dilute stock-specific risk and to enlarge the number of potentially winning stocks.

At a time of margin compression, one danger that investors need to be aware of is that the number of potential winning stocks might be small. They could therefore form an investment subset too limited to effectively diversify risk, especially since – with the end of the credit boom and central banks out of ammunition – we are going to be back in an environment where companies will find it easier to fail.

There are three strategies to minimise the dangers here.

1. Have an open-minded attitude to the investment universe

There is great advantage to having a wide investment universe. There may be fewer companies that qualify as attractive investments in the future – so it pays to be more open-minded and to be willing to invest in AIM- and ISDX-listed companies.

At present most professional investors tend to avoid researching the very smallest quoted companies on the basis that their minimal scale means that their institutions won't be able to invest millions into these stocks. In the past, when market returns have been plentiful, this thinking didn't greatly dilute investment returns. However, at a time when there are fewer winners, this attitude effectively rules out a large number of quoted businesses from consideration – irrespective of their investment merits or the scale of their upside potential.

There are 350 companies included in the mainstream mid- and larger companies index in the UK. **So professional investors that rule out all UK quoted companies that fall below a market capitalisation of around £180m**[47] **effectively exclude potentially winning investments in around 600 to 700 quoted businesses from their consideration.**[48]

Of course, there will be some winning stocks within the FTSE 350 every year – but at a time when market returns are sub-normal they might amount to a small minority. For a portfolio limited to the FTSE 350 to succeed in such a year it would need laser-like stock selection skills, avoiding nearly every stock that falls in absolute terms – and yet still accurately select most of the stocks that prove to be successful. Consistent investment success is difficult in normal market conditions; at times of economic and market stress it is even harder.

Worse still, a very short list of holdings implies relatively high portfolio weightings in preferred stocks and this raises issues with stock-specific risk. The huge sell-off in the BP share price that took place after the Deepwater Horizon oil spill in 2010 underlines the problem of excessive stock-specific risk. When the spill took place, the event was a shock to the BP management team as well as its external shareholders and went on to cost the company some $18 billion in settlements.[49] Some downside risks simply cannot be forecast. A strategy that involves a limited

---

47   The market capitalisation of the smallest member of the FTSE 350 Index was £188m, as at 30 September 2016. Source: FTSE.

48   This figure includes companies that form part of the mainstream LSE listed stocks, plus those quoted on the AIM and ISDX exchanges.

49   *BP reaches $18.7 billion settlement over deadly 2010 spill.* Source: Reuters, 3 July 2015.

number of holdings also embraces considerable portfolio volatility. It is important to widen the opportunity set to dilute stock-specific risk and to enlarge the number of potentially winning stocks.

The most common method of risk mitigation involves selecting from the widest opportunity set of potential holdings. This can also be achieved to some extent via diversification into other national markets, increasing the number of stocks available in the best performing sectors. Another approach involves identifying larger stocks excluded from mainstream indices in the UK for various reasons. This might include those companies that have demerged from larger UK quoted companies, or those that are sizeable but quoted on different exchanges, such as AIM. My previous book – *The Future is Small* – suggested that investors should widen their portfolios to more of a multi-cap stance by increasing their holdings of the smallest quoted stocks, most particularly those quoted on AIM.

2. Multi-layered management nightmares

Investors can also reduce the risk of picking poor investments by looking out for those companies with management structures that are too multi-layered.

Mainstream businesses often tend to have a number of layers of management. Unfortunately, this can end up insulating some of the business leaders from having a full understanding of the underlying problems in a business or its deficiencies. The greater the management hierarchy between the individual engaging with the customer and the individual who makes policy decisions, the longer it can take for business decisions to be made. We have all had painful conversations with call centre staff who would like to deliver the right solution to sort out our problem but can't because of some policy decision made remotely.

In many of the most responsive quoted companies, the same individual covers both the business management decisions and the customer interaction roles. The directors of many smaller quoted companies are often fully involved in both delivering products to their customers as well as making management decisions. It is worth emphasising that some larger businesses can be very effective in this area as well. This is most frequently found in businesses that have been driven by a single entrepreneur, such as Steve Jobs, the former CEO at Apple Inc.

In short, businesses with weightier management structures often have less agility. Therefore it is worth putting in some time to assess the agility of management structures. Some time on the internet can reveal poor customer experience but also those companies that are very slow at making corporate decisions.

3. Management teams and operational efficiency

Ideally a management team should have some charisma. There are other factors that are important, such as operational efficiency, but ultimately a good business is often down to clear and effective leadership.

Directors need to be knowledgeable about their customers in order to be good at inspiring the wider organisation to be effective at delivery. This often boils down to a management team that is unusually effective at explaining how the different parts of the business work together. This is an area where good detail is required. The team needs to be effective at navigating the full range of industry challenges.

Often the best opportunities for investors to assess these factors is when the leadership team present the company to shareholders. Clearly the best presentation doesn't necessarily equate with those that are best at managing their businesses. Some genuinely good management teams may not have the most polished shareholder presentations – it is an area of subtlety. Nevertheless, weak presentations are always a good indicator of management teams that have weak leadership skills. Weed out those teams who are unable to articulate the detail of their operations well.

And be alert for shareholder presentations that appear too smooth or sanitised. They might sound good in the context of a presentation but may not necessarily hold up well under detailed questioning. Ideally investors should have the opportunity to ask searching questions about business specifics to get a really clear idea of the true underlying strengths of a management team and its operations. It is particularly

CHAPTER TWELVE: RISK REDUCTION

important to identify those where the presentational gloss is only skin deep. Either way, it is an indicator of an absence of management engagement in the underlying operations of the business. Or it may suggest there is a communication weakness in the management team as a whole.

*   *   *

Ultimately, at a time of margin compression, investors need to be even more attentive to risk. The average company is likely to be under pressure and there is a chance that many will disappoint. Only the very best have a really good chance of bucking the wider trend. It is easy to get over-excited about a company with positive prospects and take on too much stock-specific risk. So be sensitive as to those management teams that are running their business in the way you would run it were it to be your role. In particular, it is well worth favouring those management teams that are particularly charismatic in leading their staff, and those that demonstrate a really good understanding of optimising operational efficiencies. Both help to reduce stock-specific risk.

The Changing Face of Finance

Productivity improvement and outstanding service standards will become two of the cornerstones of portfolio construction in future.

The exceptional returns of globalisation...

For many decades it has paid investors to assume that present trends will persist into the future. The historic pattern within markets has been in place for a generation. Stock markets may have fluctuated, but the long-term trajectory of the financial world has tended to be relatively consistent. There might have been serious market setbacks in 2000 or even 2008 but these were followed by strong recoveries. Nearly all assets have appreciated well over the years. The housing market and equity markets are probably the most obvious – but the same trend included government bonds, fine wine and artwork. Returns have been plentiful with even mundane index funds offering attractive returns year after year.

This has been driven by globalisation. The liberalisation of global trade generated an unusually vibrant period of economic growth. Alongside this, the deregulation of the debt markets increased our inclination to borrow. Extra borrowing drove down the savings ratio in most developed economies and this drove up corporate profit margins as well as supercharging economic growth.

... and its exceptional drawbacks

Globalisation might have delivered an exceptional period of stock market returns – but it has come with drawbacks too. The growing level of company takeovers has forced most quoted corporates to adopt a more 'risk on' attitude. In an ever-rising market, risk comes to look benign. Those that retained a slower but safer growth strategy found that they were vulnerable to being taken over by others with more cavalier attitudes. Those who were too cautious have been displaced by those with higher risk appetites. Prior to 2008 this culture encouraged the fastest growth sectors to expand at breakneck speed, with many quoted companies becoming greatly overextended.

The sheer scale of the Global Financial Crisis underlined just how deeply entrenched this 'risk on' culture had become. The magnitude of financial risks was so vast that it endangered the viability of the entire capitalist system. Most major banks had become so overextended that only national governments were large enough to fund their emergency needs. And the debt markets themselves became gridlocked, to the extent that only enormous amounts of extra liquidity from central banks could prevent an economic depression.

Alongside injections of financial liquidity, interest rates were reduced to 'emergency' levels in all developed markets. Central banks introduced QE to reduce the cost of funding long-term corporate debt. These policies saved many corporates from the risk of failure during the 2008 setback, but inadvertently smoothed the way for the culture of indebtedness to persist. The increase in regulation and capital ratios might have injected renewed prudence into the banking sector, but the pro-cyclical culture within most other corporates has remained largely in place.

Whilst the government and central bank policies might have boosted market returns since 2008, this has not been matched with a regular economic recovery. Therefore governments and central banks have resorted to additional stimuli every time there has been a setback. One of the problems with these policies is that they have continued to defer corporate decay. In the end, holding back the immature and more vibrant firms has the effect of distorting the corporate landscape so that it is dominated by the sedentary. It's not just about those that become overextended, or those over-dependent on ultra-low borrowing costs. It's also about many management teams simply becoming too remote from commercial imperatives.

In the past, this hasn't been especially critical because corporate margins tend to rise towards the end of boom phases. Note how they have doubled over the last three decades. But over recent years the situation has become more stretched. The fact is that investment in capital expenditure has been very limited since 2008, and this is now manifesting itself in a lack of growth in corporate cash flow. Unfortunately, over recent years many quoted companies have inadvertently moved into a position where they are over-distributing annual dividends. Since growth remains slow around the world, this stretch is now beginning to come through in a series of dividend cuts amongst FTSE 100 companies and beyond.

For now, QE has continued to drive long-term bond yields down, and hence market valuations higher. For now, the wider economic and cash flow concerns haven't greatly worried markets. For now, the previous market status quo is still just about in place, and still reflecting the trends of the past. But all this is coming to an end. Just once in a while the status quo is usurped by a major change in social attitudes. And this is happening right now. Note how most political commentators have been wrong-footed by a series of electoral results that have bucked the conventional wisdom – and demonstrated how the mind of the electorate has hardened against globalisation.

All this marks a decisive moment for investors.

Up to 2016 the best investment returns have been made by backing the status quo. But the trends of the past have come to an end. New social attitudes are already displacing the previous long-term political norms. Brexit wasn't a protest vote; it was just a more obvious data point on a new social trajectory. The election of President Trump marks another, so the new trend is now more established. Social attitudes have profoundly changed. And inevitably a major change in political attitudes leads to substantial change in future economic and market trends. Get used to it.

All this prompts a simple question: if the previous status quo is now breaking down, what are the best investment strategies for the future?

Forthcoming challenges for index funds

Our collective problem is that in spite of the huge economic setback in 2008, few businesses have used the recovery to become more resilient to the challenges ahead. A key problem with periods of economic growth is that markets tend to cull too few of the moribund. So at the end of a period of growth there are too many fragile and overextended companies, which then turn out to be vulnerable at a time of corporate retrenchment. If anything, the use of ultra-low interest rates and QE every time there is a wobble has actually increased the vulnerability of the quoted corporate sector.

There are major risks overseas too. The world recession in 2008 interrupted China's plans for ongoing employment growth. Investing in extra infrastructure was anticipated to put China in an even better position to grow employment in future. But large increases in capital expenditure have drawbacks too, especially when they're concentrated in a narrow geography and a limited range of industry sectors – the result is capital misallocation. The huge sums spent on infrastructure have left the Chinese economy with empty homes and overcapacity – and no realistic prospect of being able to repay an extraordinarily rapid accumulation of debt secured on these assets.

Most central banks have already used most of their monetary firepower addressing the problems of the previous Global Financial Crisis. Far from central banks being all powerful, the reality is that they are running short of monetary and fiscal ammo.

It is time for all savers and investors to become much more attentive to downside risk.

In future investment strategies will need to be a lot more selective since stock market averages now carry so much more risk than before. And few appreciate quite how insensitive index funds are regarding stock-specific risk. This just isn't the time to buy funds that have no conviction in their 8% holdings. Alongside this, ultra-low bond yields imply that prospective market returns will be sub-normal as well. And market volatility may be more challenging in future. All three factors imply that investors should therefore greatly reduce their use of all passive fund structures in future.

Nutrients in the forest

Woodland and rainforests are stable ecosystems because they have a good balance of growth and decay. Growth is facilitated by decay because it liberates nutrients for the more vigorous to reuse. Decay comes together with growth, in a balanced mix of maturity and vitality. As mature trees age, they rot as their vitality ebbs away. In time, it is the collapse of ancient trees that starts the process of bringing through the more vigorous, by releasing nutrients for subsequent generations. But even more importantly, the gaps left in the canopy allow light to come in to the less mature, helping some of the most vibrant to enjoy a period of unusually rapid growth.

The problem with the financial world is that the mix of growth and decay is rarely as well-balanced. At the end of sustained periods of growth, the well-established and mature are typically overly represented, because the sedentary and aged rarely fail during periods of expansion. But inevitably there are economic fluctuations, and these tend to finally destabilise the fragile and overextended, prompting periods of corporate retrenchment.

Extraneous factors might have stayed the normal seasonal pattern over recent decades, with our financial forest fixed in growth mode for an extended period. Without regular winters, growth and decay move more and more out of balance.

Currently the lack of corporate retrenchment is greatly frustrating the expansionary potential of the vigorous and immature.

But with social attitudes and economic trends on the turn, we can be more confident that the regular economic cycle will return. It may feel like moving from the vigour of a rainforest to the seasonal cycles of a temperate woodland. But it also marks a time when investment strategies will change decisively.

The decisions made by professional investors as to the changes they make to their clients' asset allocation will have a hand in driving the forthcoming trends in the wider economy. Reallocating a portion of their clients capital towards the vibrant and immature will prepare them for a period when the woodland canopy opens up due to corporate casualties. The success of this policy will not only come through in more attractive returns for savers and investors, but also the additional employment, extra domestic growth and government tax take that these kinds of stocks should generate. Few appreciate how much the financial sector can contribute in terms of being socially useful without undermining potential investment returns.

Widening the opportunity set

During the latter days of the boom, an increasing portion of our collective capital has been allocated with reference to the largest weightings in exchange indices. This not only boosted the valuations of those firms that had got super-sized, but it also narrowed the investment universe.

In future, at a time when fewer companies will be thriving, it will become advantageous to widen the investment universe. Investors with a narrow investment universe won't have a sufficiently balanced mix of the vibrant and the immature, and these portfolios could end up carrying too much downside risk. At a time of global stagnation, it is more important than ever to select individual companies that have the best chances of accessing additional risk capital irrespective of size, industry sector and index weighting. Quoted companies will have real advantages over private businesses since risk capital will be scarcer, but equally the penalty for error will be more severe. So going forward investment strategies will be determined with a much greater attention on the individual advantages and risks of each holding. And alongside this investment strategies will increasingly favour multi-capitalisation (multi-cap) funds.

With these strategies, many of the holdings in these portfolios will fall into two groups: those with attractive prospects for productivity improvement and those delivering outstanding customer service on a commercial basis.

Productivity improvement

Stepping away from market indices will have a profound impact on portfolios. It's not just that index constituents won't define the investment universe any longer. As the savings ratio starts to move back to previous norms, there is a greater risk of companies enduring wide-ranging corporate margin pressure along with stagnant economic growth. Going forward, it is time to prioritise genuine supply-side reform over extra growth, selecting for investments that are engaging in meaningful productivity improvement. After all, the best investments won't necessarily be companies with the highest growth prospects, as limiting absolute risk will be much more important to investors. Companies with safer corporate strategies will often be preferable, especially those with the potential to take advantage of iterative improvement and organic opportunity.

And those with scope to step up capital expenditure will become greatly favoured, because this will generate attractive cash payback. Cash in for more cash out. The great advantage of productivity improvements is that the cash return on the capital often comes back within a relatively short time period too. Better still, the value of that investment often persists and generates further cash flow thereafter. So at a time when dividend growth may be very limited, these kinds of investments could justify much higher market ratings. Productivity improvement will become one of the cornerstones of investment strategies in the future.

Outstanding service

Service standards often lead profitability in a commercial operation. At a time of a profits recession, companies with the usual levels of service will tend to report lower margins. Therefore investment strategies will prioritise selecting corporates with outstanding levels of customer service. At a time when world growth is very limited, these kinds of companies will be better placed to continue to generate attractive cash flow at a time when most others are under pressure.

The big question is how can investors identify the companies that are really delivering first-rate service, from those that say they are? It is only those genuinely delivering exceptional service that have a good chance of holding on to their premium profit margins whilst other competitors are cutting their prices.

Many companies use the percentage of products delivered in full and on time or the incidence of complaints as a key measure of customer service. These are useful measures to compare service levels across a sector, and to some degree across industry sectors too. But the more informative questions cover how companies assess how well customer service information is compiled to ensure that good management decisions are made. For example, how much of a company's monthly board pack is made up of details regarding service levels? The absolute level of customer service is informative, but the really interesting data relates to how much that level fluctuates over time. In general, the best businesses not only sustain their service at a high level but find ways to continuously improve. Companies with attractive profit margins then have the advantage of extra corporate cash flow that can be used to fund capital expenditure and ongoing growth. Expect outstanding service standards to become a second cornerstone of investment strategies in future.

Globalisation in retreat

Globalisation has been running into headwinds for a while. What few of us appreciated was that it had already passed its high-water mark, with the implication that market risks have been becoming more immediate. So the conclusions of this book should stand alongside the normal prudence of stock-selection priorities, favouring those with robust balance sheets, a sensible valuation at purchase, and ideally the prospect of an attractive dividend yield in future years.

But alongside this the previous social and political norms have changed decisively. For those in doubt, Brexit should be seen in the context of the hardening of attitudes around the world. Following the election of President Trump, the evidence is now overwhelming that the long-term economic trajectory has changed, and markets are in a period of flux. As others come to these conclusions, investment strategies will change more in the coming three years than they have over the last three decades.

Going forward, investment strategies will become more defined around the outcomes they seek, rather than the indices of the past. Capital will move away from index funds and ETFs, towards a wider opportunity set of stocks. Many will be multi-cap funds with a real emphasis on challenger companies that will be well-placed to take advantage of market voids left by corporate casualties. In future more equity capital will be allocated on a company-by-company basis (rather than with reference to indices), to those with the best potential to generate an attractive cash payback on productivity improvements. Alongside this, companies delivering outstanding customer service will be equally favoured, since they too will be well-positioned to sustain corporate margins at a time when many others are under real pressure.

With globalisation in retreat, this is the time when the investment industry is unusually well-placed to demonstrate just how socially useful it can be. Adopting new investment strategies like those outlined above won't just deliver premium returns to clients. The success of these strategies will also be measured in the more wide-ranging metrics of additional employment, better domestic growth and extra tax take for governments.

Bibliography

Apple reports first quarterly sales drop since 2003 as iPhone stumbles. 26 April 2016. Wall Street Journal.

Are share buybacks jeopardising future growth? October 2015. McKinsey & Company.

Bailey, A. *The capital adequacy of banks: today's issues and what we have learnt from the past.* 10 July 2014. Prudential Regulation Authority.

Bank of England will take action on buy-to-let mortgages, says Carney. 16 December 2015. Reuters.

Bank of England says market may be underpricing risks of falling liquidity. 1 October 2015. Bloomberg.

Bank of England Foreign Exchange Survey 2015. Bank of England.

Barnett, A., Batten, S., Chui, A., Franklin, J. and Sebastia-Barriel, M. *The UK productivity puzzle.* Q2 2014. Bank of England Quarterly Bulletin.

BP reaches US$18.7bn settlement over deadly 2010 spill. 3 July 2015. Thomson Reuters.

Buttiglione, B., Lane, P., Reichlin, L. and Reinhart, V. *Deleveraging, What deleveraging?* 2014. International Center for Monetary and Banking Studies.

China: Diversification Flows Drive Capital A/C. 22 February 2016. Andrew Hunt Economics.

China: Size matters. 26 March 2014. iMFdirect.

Consumer Prices in the UK: Explaining the decline in real consumer prices for cars and clothing and footwear. March 2015. Cambridge Econometrics.

Credit excesses – and busts – that we have known. 13 May 2016. Andrew Hunt Economics.

Credit Suisse Global Equity Strategy. 2016 Outlook: Themes, Sectors and Styles.

Europe's negative yields seep into non-government bond sales. 8 March 2016. Bloomberg.

Fawley, B.W. and Neely, C.J. *Four Stories of Quantitative Easing. Federal Reserve Bank of St. Louis Review,* January/February 2013, 95(1), pp. 51–88.

Family Food 2014. Department for Environment, Food and Rural Affairs (DEFRA).

Global Productivity Growth Stuck in the Slow Lane with No Signs of Recovery in Sight. Productivity Brief 2015. US Conference Board.

Goldman says commodity rally is a false start that's set to fizzle. 8 March 2016. Bloomberg.

Gore, G. *The fall and (partial) rise of RBC.* IFR Review of the Year 2012. Source: International Financing Review.

Hartnett, M. *The seven year glitch, top trumps and the Eurovision bear contest.* March 2016. Bank of America Merrill Lynch.

Hedge funds just had their worst quarter since the crisis. 18 December 2015. Bloomberg.

Kellingley closure ends deep coal mining in Britain. 17 December 2015. Reuters.

OECD Employment Outlook 2016. July 2016. OECD.

Pharmaceuticals: Value over volume. 24 September 2015. Financial Times.

Riley, J. and Chote, R. *Crisis and consolidation in public finances.* September 2014. Office for Budgetary Responsibility.

Reich, R. *Saving Capitalism: For the many, not the few.* 2015. Penguin Random House.

Reaping what you sow. May 2016. Andrew Hunt Economics.

Survey and Research Center for China Household Finance. 2014. South Western University of Finance and Economics, China.

The Road to Perdition. 11 July 2016. The MacroStrategy Partnership.

UK Dividends: Take Cover! Panmure Gordon. November 2015.

World Energy Investment Outlook. 2014 Special Report. International Energy Agency, France.

World Trade Organisation Annual Report. A year in review. 2014.

Why dynamic pricing is a must for ecommerce retailers. 18 August 2014. Econsultancy.

Index

A

Aldi 82, 83–4
Apple 82, 100
asset allocation strategies
    anxiety in 70–1
    and changing economic trends 13,
      73–4, 76–9, 108
    and corporate efficiency 75–6
    and falling bond yields 71–3
    for future markets 74–5
    outcome-orientated 75
assets
    gearing of 24
    returns on 4, 72, 85–7, 103
    valuation 24, 72

B

Bank of England 59, 60
banks
    central 28–9, 40, 48, 59–60, 63,
      66–7, 104–6
    Chinese 32, 33, 37, 38
    overextension 46–7, 104
    regulations 31
    and risk 28–9
BlackBerry 81
bond yields
    low 1, 105–6
    negative returns 66, 67
    reduction in 16–17, 60, 71–2, 73
booms and busts 45–7, *see also* credit
    boom
borrowing, consumer 21
BP 98
Brazil 37

Brexit (referendum) 1, 6–7, 105, 110

C

capital
  Chinese expenditure 34–6
  and dotcom stocks 70
  dual structures 23–4, 26
  easy access to 24, 43, 108
  expenditure on energy 53
  increases 106
  lack of 63–4, 105
  and productivity improvement 43,
    61, 63–4, 67, 86–9, 109–11
  structures 26–7
  trading volumes 18
car industry 20–1
cash flow
  and capital investment 63–4, 67, 75
  and cash payback periods 90, 109
  growth 51, 61–2
  and high service level companies
    95, 110
  lack of growth in 48, 53–5, 105
  and productivity improvement
    86–9
cash payback periods 90, 109
central banks 28–9, 40, 48, 59–60, 63,
  66–7, 104–6
change
  in financial markets 1–2

  in investment strategies 67–8,
    69–79, 105–11
  in social attitudes 1, 55–6, 73, 105–6,
    110–11
China
  banks 32, 33, 37, 38
  capital expenditure 34–6
  credit boom 32–41
  debt 38–41
  economic growth 32–4
  housing market 36
  infrastructure investment 33–7, 60,
    67, 106
City of London 17
clothing industry 9–10
coal industry 9
commodities 34, 36–7, 52
companies see quoted companies
complacency 40
complaints 93–5
Conservative Party 6
consumers 56–8
Corbyn, Jeremy 6
corporate culture 23–4, 25–7, 29
corporate efficiency 21, 27, 75–6, 100–1
corporate failure 48, 77, 78
corporate profits see also profit
  margins
    growth in 15–22
    and productivity improvement
      88–90

recovery in 61
corporate profit share 19–20
'creative destruction' theory 44–5, 47
credit boom
    and capital investment 86–7
    and change in corporate culture
      23–5
    changes leading to 11–12
    Chinese 32–41
    and economic growth 51
    and financial market trends 12–14
    and financial services sector 17
    and fund management sector 26–7
    and the Global Financial Crisis
      27–9
    impact on corporate profits 19–22
customers
    complaints 93–5
    and premium pricing 92
    pressure on profit margins 64
customer service
    measurement of 93–5, 110
    outstanding 109–10, 111

D

debt
    for corporate expansion 16
    in corporate structure 88
    easy access to 43, 76
    funding of 29, 76–7, 104
    growth of Chinese 33, 37–41, 106

    and rise in equity prices 17–18
    use of more 21, **23–9**
debt markets
    Chinese 38
    deregulation of 11, 16, 71, 104
    and the Global Financial Crisis
      28–9
    gridlock 104
    innovation in 17
decay
    concept of growth and 43–4, 107–8
    in the financial sector 44–5
    problem of lack of 47
deflation, through globalisation 11, 71
dividend cover 61–2, 64–6
dividend growth strategy 75
dotcom boom 70
dual capital structure 23–4, 26

E

economic cycles 2
economic growth
    disappointment in 63–6
    impact of globalisation 11
    lack of 54–5
economic recovery
    disappointment in 63–6
    lack of 66–8
    opportunity for 61–3
    policy for after the Global
      Financial Crisis 59–60

economy
  in aggregate 21
  booms and busts 45–7
  growth and decay concept 43–4
  impact of globalisation 8–11
  problem of lack of decay 47
  trends 69–70
emerging economies 34, 36–7
energy, and corporate profit margins
  52–3, 55–6
equity income funds 74
equity markets *see* financial markets
European Economic Community 8
European Exchange Rate Mechanism
  12
European Union, impact of leaving 78
exchange rates, sterling 12
exchange-traded funds (ETFs) 77, 111

F

finance, change in 1–2, 103–11
financial markets
  change in 1–2
  control 67, 104–5
  deregulation 45–6
  returns 4, 15–16, 45–6, 63–6, 72, 103
  risks 104, 110–11
  trends 70
financial sector
  growth and decay 44–5, 107–8
  as niche 84

financial services industry 17–18
food
  fall in household spend on 57
  retail as niche 84
foreign exchange, trading volumes 18
FTSE 350 index 98
fund management 26–7, 70, 78
Future is Small, The (Williams) 1, 99

G

Global Financial Crisis
  and Chinese infrastructure
    investment 34
  and corporate growth trend 53–5
  and the credit boom 27–9
  and 'risk on' culture 104
globalisation
  consumer attitudes towards 53–5
  and corporate profit growth 15–18
  deflationary 71
  drawbacks of 40–1, 104–6
  economic boom 45–6
  and financial markets 1, 12–14
  and market risks 110
  political trends as a reaction to 6–7
  returns of 103–4
  social attitudes towards 7
  and stock market growth 16
government bonds 60, 67
government expenditure 60

Greece 54, 62–3
Green Party 5
growth and decay
    balance between **43–9**
    concept of 43–4, 107–8
    corporate 2
    in the financial sector 44–5

H

health, as niche 84
Hegel, Georg 44
holdings, dangers of limited numbers
    of 98–9
housing market 24, 25, 36

I

import tariffs, UK 8
income growth strategy 74–5
index funds 2, 72–3, 75, 77, 107, 111
industry, as niche 84
inflation, and deregulation 11
infrastructure investment, Chinese
    33–7, 60, 67, 106
institutional investment 24, 70–1,
    85–6
interest rates
    and currencies 37
    decline in 11–12
    keeping low 28–9, 40, 63, 66, 78
    negative 66

    reduction in 47–8, 59–60, 63, 76,
        104, 106
    rise in 11–12
internal rate of return (IRR) 89
international trade barriers 8–9, 32
investment
    infrastructure 33–7, 60, 67, 106
    institutional 24, 70–1, 85–6
    universe 97–9, 108–9
investment industry, socially useful
    111
investment strategies
    and aggregate risks in equity
      markets **59–68**
    based on outstanding service 91–2,
      109–10
    based on past long-term trends
      3–4, 103–6
    based on productivity
      improvement 63, 74–7, 79, 85–90,
      109
    change in **69–79**, 105–6, 110–11
    in companies in mainstream
      indices 85–6
    selective 107–9
    with a widened opportunity set
      97–101

J

Japan 47–8

job creation, impact of globalisation
    8–10
Jobs, Steve 100

L

Labour Party 6, 55
leisure, as niche 84
Lewis, Dave 76
Lidl 82, 83–4
liquidity
    easy access to 76
    injections of 60, 104

M

management 99–101
manufacturing 8
market capitalisation 15–16
markets *see* financial markets
Marks & Spencer 82, 83
media sector 10–11
mergers and acquisitions 25–7
Microsoft 82
multi-capitalisation funds 99, 108, 111
multinationals 66, 72–3

N

nationalism, political trends towards
    6–7
negative interest rates 66
niches **81–4**

Nokia 81

O

oil prices 37, 53
operational efficiency 75–6, 100–1
outcome-orientated investment
    strategies 75–6
outstanding service companies
    109–10

P

pension schemes 66
pharmaceutical industry 10, 56
politics
    pressure on profit margins 55–6
    and social change 5–7
    trends in 5–7
price wars 57–8
private equity 25
pro-cyclical culture 29
productivity
    improvement **85–90**, 109
    investment for growth 63–4
    lack of improvement in 48–9, 67
    need to prioritise 78–9
    slowing 73–4
profit margins
    consumer pressure on 56–8, 64
    and the credit boom 21
    decline in 51–3

expansion 17

high 76

and high service level companies
91–2, 109–10

and political pressure 55–6

rise in 19, 23

and the savings ratio 104, 109

stretched 105

profit share, corporate 19–20

profits recession **51–8**

Q

quantitative easing (QE) 28, 34, 54, 63,
66–7, 104, 105

quoted companies 63–4, 98–9, 105,
106

R

returns on assets 4, 72, 85–7, 103

risk
corporate 26–9, 77–9, 89–90, 104

investment **59–68**, 72–5, 106–10

reduction strategies **97–101**

regulations to prevent 31

Royal Bank of Scotland 46

S

savings ratio, and profit margins 21–2,
51–2, 104, 109

Schumpeter, Joseph 44, 47

Scottish National Party 6

SDP 5

service standards
leading profitability 109–10

premium for premium returns
91–5

shareholding structure, dual 23–4, 26

Slow Finance (Williams) 1, 17–18

small companies 83–4, 98–9, 105

social attitudes
change in 1, 4–8, 55–6, 105–6, 108

and slowing productivity 73–4

stagnation 47–9, 54

sterling, devaluation 12, 54, 57, 72

stimulus
after the Global Financial Crisis
59–60

from central banks 104–5

running out of 66–8

stockmarkets *see* financial markets

stock-specific risk 98–9

'sublation' 44

supermarkets sector 57–8, 82

T

takeovers 23–4, 104

technology
innovation in 20–1

as niche 84

stocks 81–2

Tesco 58, 76

Thatcher, Margaret 8
trade
    China's growing share of global
      32–4
    globalisation 40, 45, 53
    liberalisation of 8–9, 11–12, 16, 20,
      104
Trump, Donald 1, 6–7, 73, 106, 111

U

Unilever 58
United Kingdom
    budget deficit 60, 67
    corporate profit share 18–22
    economic recovery 61–2
    falling bond yields 71–3
    financial services industry 15–18
    impact of globalisation 8–11
    lack of economic growth 63–8
    lack of productivity improvement
      48–9
    leaving of EU 7, 78
    profits recession 51–8
    risk of economic stagnation 48–9
    social change in the 5–11
    stimulating recovery 48, 59–60
United States 19–20, 52
utility suppliers 55–6

V

video games development 10–11

W

wage growth 8–9, 54–5, 64
Waitrose 82
wealth creation 8–9, 86
workplace regulation, as niche 84
world growth slowdown 28, 34, 40,
    53–4, 63–4, 74

The Future is Small

Why **AIM** will be the world's best market beyond the credit boom

"I heartily recommend this volume to any reader who is willing to decide for themselves how to deploy their savings."

– Luke Johnson, Chairman, Risk Capital Partners

"… what makes Gervais really quite fascinating is that Gervais obviously thinks big. He's interested in fixing big problems, that impact all of us at the national level, and help produce nasty surprises within our investment portfolios…"

– David Stevenson, *FT* Columnist, editor of *Portfolio Review* and consultant

"This seems as good a time as any to mention – indeed to recommend as a stocking-filler – a new book called *The Future is Small*, which is written by one of the City's most respected fund managers, Gervais Williams … he produces some stunning statistics to back up his case."

– Anthony Hilton, *Evening Standard*

"It's a fascinating read for anyone keen to exploit the investment potential of the UK's thriving small business environment."

– Faith Glasgow, *Money Observer*

I N a financial world dominated by gigantism, the beauty of smallness hasn't had much of a look in. Yet beyond the credit boom, globalisation has been found wanting, with growth hard to find. Could it be that small firms are set to be the stock market outperformers of the future?

The Future is Small confounds the current 'big is better' consensus, with Gervais Williams' extraordinary data showing why smallness offers an effective path for investors beyond the financial crisis.

But this book is about so much more than just the case for small being beautiful. It also explains why the unique characteristics of AIM – the UK market for smaller, growing companies – will be a place of extraordinary vitality in the coming years.

www.harriman-house.com/the-future-is-small

THANKS
FOR READING!

Our readers mean everything to us at Harriman House. As a special thank-you for buying this book let us help you save as much as possible on your next read:

If you've never ordered from us before, get £5 off your first order at **harriman-house.com** with this code: rog551

Already a customer? Get £5 off an order of £25 or more with this code: rog25

Get 7 days' FREE access to hundreds of our books at **volow.co** – simply head over and sign up.

Thanks again!
from the team at